WORK
WITHOUT
WALLS

An Executive's Guide to
Attention Management, Productivity,
and the Future of Work

MAURA NEVEL THOMAS

Burget Ave
PRESS
Austin, TX

Published by
Burget Ave Press
Austin, TX

Publisher's Cataloging-in-Publication Data
Thomas, Maura Nevel.

   Work without walls : an executive's guide to attention management, productivity, and the future of work / Maura Nevel Thomas. – Austin, TX : Burget Ave Press, 2017.

   p. ; cm.

   ISBN13: 978-0-9980095-0-6

   1. Industrial management. 2. Industrial productivity. 3. Success in business. I. Title.

HD31.2.T46 2017
658—dc23   2016955264

FIRST EDITION

Project coordination by Jenkins Group, Inc.
www.jenkinsgroupinc.com

Cover design: Elizabeth Sheehan

Front cover photograph: Shawn P. Thomas, Fine Art Photographer, Infinite View Images, www.infiniteviewimages.com

Interior design: Yvonne Fetig Roehler

Interior infographics: Stephanie Johnson

Printed in the United States of America
21   20   19   18   17 • 5   4   3   2   1

WORK

WITHOUT

WALLS

Also by Maura Nevel Thomas

Personal Productivity Secrets: Do What You Never Thought Possible with Your Time and Attention...and Regain Control of Your Life!

This book is dedicated to
the CEOs and leaders with whom I've worked throughout the life
of my business, and specifically in my speaking for Vistage International.
I appreciate the Chairs who have invited me into their groups,
and the staff at Vistage headquarters who coordinate the engagements.
These clients have been invaluable to me in shaping and refining
the contents of this book.

It is also dedicated to my husband, Shawn,
whose endless support, patience, love, and partnership
make every part of my life easier and more enjoyable.

CONTENTS

Introduction

CORPORATE America has been experiencing a shift. In some ways it seems like the business environment is changing quickly, but in reality this shift has been gradual. In fact, Peter Drucker, widely recognized as the founder of modern management, predicted this shift as early as the 1950s, but the realization of his predictions has taken decades to manifest. The shift is both endlessly discussed and almost completely ignored. The shift to which I'm referring is the shift from industrial work to knowledge work.

In the Industrial Age, work happened within the walls of a factory. Today, knowledge work is the product of our brains. Increasingly, that work has left the confines of an office. Companies have moved to cubicle environments and open floor plans. Often the work is done outside the company walls entirely because technology advancements allow knowledge workers to do their work anywhere, at any time. Traditional work relationships are changing, with freelance and contract workers making up over 40 percent[1] of the workforce, and more work happening outside the office than ever before. In addition to the loss of so many physical walls, the metaphorical walls between work time and personal time—and between work spaces and personal spaces—are "crumbling."

While technologists have been capitalizing on this shift for years, individuals are struggling to adapt their lives at work, and corporations are struggling to adapt their policies and practices, to this shift. The phrase I use to sum up the issues and challenges inherent in this shift to knowledge work is "Work Without Walls." While the phrase "knowledge work" is common vernacular, the implications for workers and the impact on company culture is a problem vexing companies of all sizes throughout the United States.

What Is Knowledge Work?

Knowledge work, for the purposes of this book, is defined as work for which "thinking" is the raw material. The products of knowledge work are communications, information, and complex decisions. In technology development, much thought has been given to automating processes and imposing structure to create more efficiency in knowledge work, and larger companies are slowly beginning to exhibit some changes, making news for their nonconformity. However, little attention has been given in smaller companies to adapt to this monumental change, or to help individuals navigate the new realities of work, the new tools available to them, and the increasingly blurred lines between "business and personal" and "work and downtime."

Although "institutional" productivity is important, the worker as a human being is a critical piece of the equation. If "thinking" is a raw material of knowledge work, then the biases in which that thinking is framed are relevant. These biases are formed by how individual knowledge workers feel about their tasks and their jobs overall and by how well the tool they use to produce the thinking—their brain—is performing. These two things mean that the workers' personal well-being should be attended to. In fact, studies show[2] that a key skill among high-performing executives is the ability to cultivate successful relationships, where leaders are seen as genuinely caring about the well-being of their colleagues.

However, there is a particular kind of company that seems to operate with the assumption that workers are disposable and a grueling work environment where people regularly cry at their desks are requirements to stay competitive and increase profits.[3] If this is the type of company you're running, then this book—which is based on the belief that healthy, happy, and productive employees are better for individuals, companies, and society at large—is not for you.

Types of Knowledge Work

There is an argument to be made that there are different types of knowledge work, and I would agree. For example, there is knowledge work for which the primary outputs are specifically the product of thinking. Writers, designers, and other creative types; senior executives in charge of ideas and strategy; and software developers are some examples of this type of knowledge worker. A broader definition of knowledge work includes more task-oriented positions, such as administrative staff. These roles still have more in common with knowledge work than manufacturing or other industrial work, so when I refer to knowledge workers, I'm including office workers in general.

Symptoms of the Shift to Knowledge Work

There are many symptoms and challenges inherent in this shift, including:

- The unique needs of knowledge work with regard to optimal functioning of our brains, such as downtime, nutrition, and overall well-being, and the attitudes and perspectives of the workers.
- The increasing importance of attention, simultaneous with the rise of endless distractions.
- The proliferation of communication and the nature of urgency that surrounds it.
- The growing importance of downtime.
- The office environment, such as open offices, privacy, noise, and collaboration.
- The rise of work outside offices, raising issues related to both the logistics of telecommuting and the expansion of work hours.
- Quantification and measurement of knowledge work.

➤ Corporate culture as it relates to the support or the detriment of all of these issues.

Because we are still in the midst of the shift and don't yet have the benefit of hindsight, there is still much contradictory information. Pick up one business magazine and you'll read that telecommuting is the wave of the future. But then you'll see another article that argues that telecommuting is terrible for workers. Open-office floor plans have been both lauded as the "silver bullet" for optimal knowledge work (innovation) and derided as the worst business concept in decades. The issues are confusing, and without an understanding of each of the challenges identified in the preceding list, leaders are at risk of leaving to chance corporate culture, employee engagement, and ultimately, productivity.

The New Rules of Work

There are new realities of our work without walls that compound this confusion. Contrary to popular belief, the following are *not* characteristics of a productive knowledge worker:

➤ Being available for work 24/7/365

➤ Maximum face time in the office

➤ Working on vacation

➤ Multitasking

➤ "I can sleep when I'm dead" attitude

➤ Busyness as a "badge of honor"

In the world of work without walls, "work-life balance" not only exists but also is critical. A result of today's work environment is that too many workers are exhausted. Exhausted workers mean exhausted companies, exhausted families, exhausted communities, and an exhausted world. The bottom line for busy professionals struggling to regain control over their lives, and for the companies that employ them, is that EXHAUSTION IS OPTIONAL, and it's not conducive to quality outcomes for knowledge work.

I believe that the way we look at work needs an overhaul. What it means to be productive is subjective and situational, but the ideas in this book are founded on my belief, from more than two decades of experience, that the individual productivity of a knowledge worker is based on the extent to which that person makes progress on his or her *significant* results in any given time frame. The productivity of a knowledge worker in the context of the larger organization must take a person's level of engagement and happiness into account. If a worker meets deadlines, produces superior results for the organization, and achieves objectives, but hates her job, is she productive? This situation is not sustainable and would likely lead to burnout, disengagement, or a departure, any of which would ultimately lower the overall productivity of the organization.

Goals of This Book

The purpose of my work is to teach busy, driven knowledge workers to regain control of their lives and work so that they can live a life of choice, and joyfully and enthusiastically offer their unique gifts (their significant results) to the world every day. It's those gifts that will power the world into a successful future and that will allow us to realize the promise of our individual and collective potential. This book is my latest effort in support of that purpose.

A great companion to this book at the individual level is my first book, Personal Productivity Secrets: Do what you never thought possible with your time and attention...and regain control of your life!

My goal in the following pages is to help leaders by taking an in-depth look at the new world of work without walls and at the specific issues that are reshaping the modern workplace. With each, I'll help you sort out the latest research and give recommendations based on my experience in the productivity industry. You'll come away with new understanding and fresh ideas that will make a real difference in your company.

In every trend addressed in this book, distraction is a common theme. The problem of distraction has many layers: the distraction itself, the response to the distraction, and the individual's habits as they relate to the distraction. These nuances have been lost in the majority of the studies and articles related to these issues, but each component of distraction has its own causes and consequences, and needs to be addressed individually and thoroughly for a complete picture of knowledge worker productivity and how to improve it.

I'd love to know how you put the information in this book to use. You can connect with me through any of the following channels:

Twitter: @mnthomas

Facebook and YouTube: /RegainYourTime

Email: info@regainyourtime.com

Phone: 424.22Maura (424.226.2872)

Thanks for reading!

Maura

MAURA THOMAS

Speaker, Trainer, Author

Founder, RegainYourTime.com

Features of This Book

THE following features and icons are used in this book to draw your attention to some of the most important and useful information and some of the most valuable tips, insights, and advice that can help you unlock the productivity at your organization.

Sidebars

Sidebars Look Like This

Sidebars provide additional information about topics related to the nearby text.

Callout Text

Callout text, example shown below, is used to emphasize text.

> *Callout text looks like this. The callout emphasizes important text.*

Margin Notes

Margin notes like this one will highlight some important piece of information, elaborate more fully on a point, or direct you to other relevant information.

Margin notes look like this.

Highlighted Text

Highlighted text adds emphasis to important information.

Each chapter includes a comprehensive "Institutional Changes" section which contains my recommendations for changes at the corporate level to address the issues raised in that chapter.

Action Items

Also included is an "Action Items" section designed to provide very specific steps that you can take.

Takeaways You Can Tweet

Also at the end of each chapter is a section called "Takeaways You Can Tweet" that contains a short summary of many of the important points in the chapter. These tips each contain fewer than 140 characters, so that they are easy to digest, but also so that you can conveniently share the information with your followers on Twitter or on other social media outlets. I'd love to know if you are finding the information worthy of sharing, so please include #workwithoutwalls and/or my username, @mnthomas, or otherwise tag me if you have room.

Chapter 1

THE "HUMAN" PART OF HUMAN CAPITAL

Knowledge-worker productivity requires that the knowledge worker is both seen and treated as an "asset" rather than a "cost." It requires that knowledge workers want to work for the organization in preference to all other opportunities.[4]

—PETER F. DRUCKER

AN underappreciated difference between knowledge workers and manufacturing workers is that their brains are the primary tool of their trade, and thinking is the primary raw material. The race for talent is increasingly a competitive one. "Skilled labor" is a media buzzword that encapsulates the situation, and "burnout" is a catch-all term for the results of neglecting this situation. No recruiters or hiring managers ask interviewees about how many emails they can answer in a day, how many hours they routinely work, or among how many things can they divide their attention. They ask about their critical-thinking skills, knowledge, and experience. These qualities give a company a competitive advantage, and the "productivity" of the individual is the extent to which a person can bring these characteristics to his or her job. Yet companies are ignoring major components of nurturing and growing this advantage. Efficiency and productivity require making the best use of the resources available. In the knowledge economy, the most important individual and corporate resources are neither time nor money, but body and mind.

There are several factors that have a daily and cumulative effect on staff well-being and performance, but these factors are typically left out of corporate engagement and wellness programs.

Corporate engagement initiatives are generally focused on outcomes such as collaboration, worker expectations, buy-in of the mission and vision, and commitment. Corporate wellness initiatives are typically focused on things like weight, blood pressure and cholesterol management, and smoking cessation. Although these programs are useful, they leave a gap in addressing productivity needs; one that could be viewed as "holistic well-being," of which attention management is a core tenet. See Figure 1.1

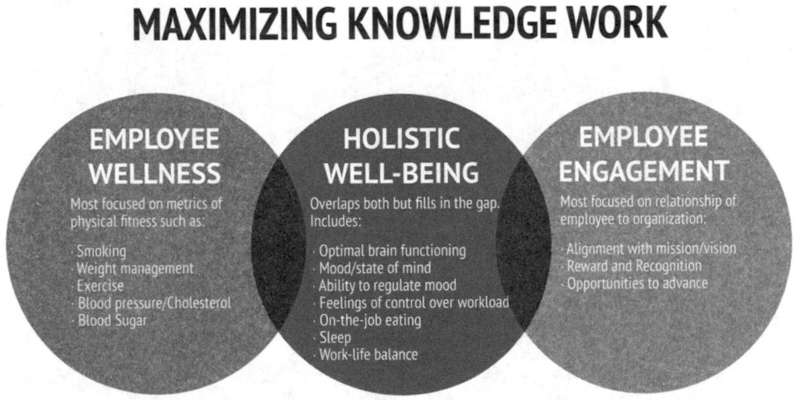

MAXIMIZING KNOWLEDGE WORK

EMPLOYEE WELLNESS
Most focused on metrics of physical fitness such as:
- Smoking
- Weight management
- Exercise
- Blood pressure/Cholesterol
- Blood Sugar

HOLISTIC WELL-BEING
Overlaps both but fills in the gap. Includes:
- Optimal brain functioning
- Mood/state of mind
- Ability to regulate mood
- Feelings of control over workload
- On-the-job eating
- Sleep
- Work-life balance

EMPLOYEE ENGAGEMENT
Most focused on relationship of employee to organization:
- Alignment with mission/vision
- Reward and Recognition
- Opportunities to advance

Figure 1.1. *Holistic Well-Being.*

Consider that 94 percent of leaders surveyed reported that the three states of mind that drive the greatest levels of effectiveness and performance are calm, happy, and energized.[5] Also, a study done in conjunction with the *Harvard Business Review* found that positive feelings about work correlated with higher engagement and higher profitability.[6]

In order to produce their best at work, knowledge workers are faced with a holistic well-being challenge to aid in feeling calm, happy, and energized. Work-life balance is a

Corporate wellness programs and engagement initiatives are great, but they still leave a gap in maximizing brain performance of knowledge workers. Not only does knowledge workers' physical fitness affect their ability to bring their best to their work, but also their mental state and mental fitness do as well.

critical component. This mental state is affected by many factors, and making small changes in the organization with this goal in mind can have a positive impact and avoid employee burnout. The company policies and practices that affect these issues typically come about without intention. Fortunately, this is a situation that is not difficult to correct.

Closing the Gap of Holistic Well-Being

You can't extend the day beyond twenty-four hours, but you can affect energy levels to improve outcomes in the same amount of time. As best-selling author and organizational psychologist Dr. Travis Bradberry writes, "Highly successful people don't skip meals, sleep, or breaks in the pursuit of more, more, more. Instead, they view food as fuel, sleep as recovery, and breaks as opportunities to recharge in order to get even more done."[7] If corporate wellness programs focus on physical wellness, and corporate engagement programs focus on the employees' relationship to their organization, the missing piece for knowledge worker productivity is every individuals' relationship with their brain (the physical functioning of the tangible organ) and their mind (the intangible outputs of brain functioning including feelings, thoughts, imagination, beliefs, and attitudes). Factors that directly affect the brain and mind include

➤ **Nutrition:** Including in-office eating and its effects on energy
➤ **Sleep:** Both quality and quantity

➤ **Control:** Perceived control over the details of work

➤ **State of mind and mindfulness:** The ability to manage one's state of mind.

Really, all the other subjects addressed in this book still indirectly affect the outputs of the brain and mind. As a leader, you can influence each of these factors.

Nutrition: Feed Employees' Success

Proper nutrition begins at home, but leadership can have a significant impact on performance factors during work hours for on-site employees. In addition to being damaging to health long term, energy roller coasters (usually caused by blood sugar highs and crashes) throughout the day are distracting and impact performance. You know that your team members are hardly at their best when fighting off the drowsy, foggy feeling associated with the crash after a sugar high. And science backs you up: studies show that people with better blood-sugar regulation perform better on cognitive tests than those with poor glucose regulation.[8]

Morning meetings often include foods high in carbohydrates and refined sugar that cause blood sugar to spike and then crash during the morning hours. Swapping bagels and pastries for egg sandwiches, breakfast tacos, or yogurt parfaits (protein-rich and low-glycemic foods) can help prevent wild swings in blood glucose. This is not only true for morning meetings but also for afternoon snacks as well. Healthy snacks offered in the break room can pay big dividends in supporting your team's energy management throughout the day. These can include baby carrots, hummus, whole wheat crackers, apple slices with peanut or other nut butter for dipping, cheese cubes or spreads, or all-natural nut bars. Invest in a filtered water source for the office, and consider stocking the fridge with flavored water drinks and natural, unsweetened teas instead of sodas, because water promotes proper hydration (another component of nutrition) and doesn't affect blood sugar. These suggestions are also useful to keep in mind for company conferences, off-site meetings, retreats, or any type of catered event.

Sleep: More Rest, More Productivity

Sleep deprivation is so widespread in the United States that the CDC considers it to be a public health problem,[9] and its effects on performance, including impaired judgment, problem-solving, and plan execution, are well documented.[10] When your employees feel tied to their devices—whether because they feel it's necessary to get ahead or because they don't know how to manage distractions— *More on this in Chapter 2.* they might be having problems getting a good night's sleep. In a survey done by *Harvard Business Review* based on my article about late-night emails (excerpted from this book), 55 percent of respondents said that late-night emailing affects their sleep and makes them less productive the next day.[11]

One way to combat the productivity drain caused by sleep deprivation is to get on board with napping at work. Everyone experiences natural fluctuations in energy throughout the day, and often a short, ten- to twenty-minute nap can be a great solution to improve performance for hours. Napping has been shown to increase alertness, improve learning and memory, increase creativity, boost productivity, improve mood, and decrease stress.[12]

Many successful companies have taken this information to heart by offering nap rooms (HubSpot, Zappos, Nike) and "energy pods" (Google, Huffington Post/AOL).[13] If you're a leader, encouraging your team members to enjoy a little shut-eye when they can, will lead to more productivity than pushing them to fill every minute with activity. Spread the word that napping is acceptable (and encouraged!) and that it's a lot more effective than the sugar- or caffeine-loading habits that are ingrained in so many office cultures.

Control: Workflow Management and Mastering Distractions

When workers feel overwhelmed, buried by email, and in a state of always having way more to do than they can ever get done, feelings of exhaustion—and often futility—interfere with their enjoyment of their job. According to the American Institute of Stress, workers who perceive they are subjected to high demands but have little control are at increased risk for cardiovascular disease.[14] These feelings of stress and overload are also a recipe for staying trapped in reactive mode, because humans are motivated by achievement, and every little email message checked or instant message responded to creates a brief but appealing sense of accomplishment, like a tiny task that is mentally (or physically) ticked off a list.

Compounding the problem is that most workers don't have the skills to manage the complexity of their lives and work. Multiple digital distractions compete with multitasking tendencies and other human distractions for employees' increasingly taxed attention in the fast-paced knowledge workplace. Productivity is lower if employees are unable to control their attention because the constant barrage of communication and information offered by their technology too easily distracts them. Attention management is the antidote to distraction, and yet most business leaders still hold antiquated ideas of "time management" that were created in the days before handheld computers and omnipresent Internet connections. Consequently, corporate training is also framed in this outdated philosophy.

The solution to the problem of your team members feeling overwhelmed and exhausted is to give them workflow-management skills that include attention management. This is covered from a leadership perspective in chapter 2, and it's also the subject of my first book, *Personal Productivity Secrets: Do what you never thought possible with your time and attention...and regain control of your life!*

State of Mind and Mindfulness: A Pause Is Powerful

A fourth component of this holistic well-being challenge is state of mind and mindfulness, which are the result of a long and complex set of variables in addition to sleep, nutrition, and workflow management. Performance is affected by not only an individual's state of mind, but also by their ability to recognize and modify their state of mind.

Alexander Caillet, an organizational psychologist on the Georgetown University faculty, conducted research along with two colleagues on how state of mind affects performance. They found that "leaders with lower states of mind, defined as frustrated, disappointed and tired, are aware of these limitations, but get trapped into repeating patterns."[15] In addition to biology, he offered two other suggestions for changing mental state: physiology and recognize/reframe/refocus. In an interview for WNY's *Money Talking*, he says:

> "The ability to stop, the ability to take a pause or to take a break, or to engage in breathing are actually ways that we can immediately shift into a quieter and clearer state of mind . . . calling out an emotion has the effect of reducing its intensity. Refocus your attention to another project. Reframe the situation by breaking it down into smaller parts that can be addressed independently."[16]

Both of these are components of mindfulness, defined by *Psychology Today* as a state of attention to the present, where thoughts and feelings are observed objectively.[17] Practicing mindfulness is a powerful way to learn to control and regulate one's emotions, thought patterns, and behaviors. Once relegated to the fringes of culture, mindfulness is now widely recognized as a necessary business skill for knowledge workers and twenty-first century leaders.

Peter Drucker brought up the idea of mindfulness in business decades ago. He taught that deep self-knowledge was a foundational skill for leaders, and he wrote an entire book (*Managing Oneself*, Harvard Business Press, 2008) about his belief that managing yourself is necessary before you can successfully manage others.

> *Mindfulness in business was first embraced by Peter Drucker, and it is now in practice at Fortune 100 companies.*

Drucker was ahead of his time. Recent research has shown that mindfulness can change your brain in positive ways,[18] and yet executives who intentionally and strategically incorporate mindfulness into their business strategy, such as Rupert Murdoch, Oprah Winfrey, and Arianna Huffington, are still in the minority. While not yet common, mindfulness in business has, in fact, gone mainstream, with companies as diverse as Google, Aetna, General Mills, and Target all having built extensive programs to foster mindful practices among their workers.[19] Consider including training and education on mindfulness in your corporate development initiatives.

Another way to change state of mind is through exercise. Exercise not only optimizes brain function, but it also affects mood, anxiety, outlook, and attention. While important to mention in this context, I won't expound on that here because this is something typically addressed in wellness programs.

Be a Role Model

Making changes to the snacks in the office kitchen and adding some spots to rest don't require a radical corporate overhaul to implement. However, none of these will be as useful as they could be without leadership buy-in and modeling of the desired behaviors. The culture of an organization is set from the top. Be intentional about behavior outcomes you want to see, and then model those behaviors yourself, like reaching for water instead of sugary drinks, choosing protein-based meals for your catered meetings, and making use of the new nap room. Leading by example sets the stage for effective change, and will be a theme repeated throughout this book.

Work-Life Balance Is Crucial

Work-life balance is a very popular topic in the media, and I've been dismayed to see a trend in statements that "work-life balance doesn't exist." It's also been suggested that "work-life balance" has become "work-life blending." Perhaps these statements are the result of experts being contrarian for attention, but I reject the notion that balance is unachievable. Not only is it possible, but also it's necessary for productive and high-quality knowledge work.

Of course, the first question that must be addressed is, "What is meant by *balance*?" I define a *balanced* life as one that includes activities that nurture not only professional desires and personal pursuits but also that puts an intentional focus on all aspects of well-being, contentment, and satisfaction, such as healthy introspection and analysis, strong social ties, hobbies, personal growth, and financial sustainability. The fact is that you can't adequately pursue any of these areas if you spend the majority of your time working.

If balance is defined this way, it's not hard to assess. Of course, it's up to you to decide whether your life is in balance, but if you routinely work while doing recreational activities, even after putting in a full workday or a full workweek, then I would say your balance is off. Technology is useful when it allows you to *replace* in-office time by keeping tabs on work while you are somewhere else, such as a doctor's office or your home. However, if your devices prolong your work time by promoting a situation where you are always somehow engaged in work, that's when the technology becomes detrimental to balance.

Juggling Work and Personal Responsibilities

You might think that your Internet-connected smartphone creates a situation where you can both work *and* attend your child's school play or soccer game, but I suggest that is simply a convenient narrative. At best, you're making a halfway effort at both your work and your attention to your child, and at worst, being there without being present might be worse than not being there at all. Your children know when they have your attention versus when they don't. And consider this regarding the struggle for presence amid technology between parents and children: If your children have to compete with your technology for your attention, and they lose, perhaps *their* single-minded focus on technology is simply their consolation prize.

When technology lengthens your workday—for example, when you come home from a full day at work, have dinner with your family, put your kids to bed, and then get back on your laptop—the time you spend working after hours is time that could be spent cultivating other interests and pursuits that would make your life more balanced. For example, you could be having a video chat with a friend, playing a game, or tackling a household or creative project with a family member, engaging in a hobby, reading, or even just relaxing in front of the television with a favorite person or a pet. (Another option is to go to bed earlier.) Any one of these activities creates opportunities for brain processes that will be beneficial to your work when you do go back to it. Games, hobbies, and other creative activities stimulate creative thinking, encourage single-tasking, clear your mind, and improve your confidence.[20] Cuddling up to another person, and even stroking a pet, releases brain-boosting endorphins that reduce stress and contribute to a feeling of well-being.[21] Laughter, like you might experience on a call with a favorite person, has similar effects.

This perspective—that technology lengthens your workday to your detriment—can be difficult to maintain in high-pressure work environments. In Silicon Valley, it's often referred to as "martyr capitalism," and is characterized by the unspoken rule of "killing it," where "if you're not sleeping under your desk, you're not committed."[22] However, as a leader, it's your job to be firm in the face of this pressure, recognizing that although it may seem like working long hours will help you get ahead, there is no research that proves that productivity increases with more than forty hours of work per week; in fact, there is ample evidence that it doesn't.[23] So if you experience any guilt about engaging in other activities instead of working, remember that often the best thing you can do *for* your work is not work!

Assessing Your Own Work-Life Balance

Insufficient attention to the holistic well-being considerations in the prior section of this chapter can provide a red flag that your work-life balance is off. Additionally, further indication may be if some or all of the following statements are true for you:

- You never take vacation, or you work when you're on vacation.

- You're never away from email for more than six or eight hours at a time.

- You are generally available to anyone regardless of the day or time.

- You never shut off your phone, or put it in "Do Not Disturb" mode.

- You have no hobbies, or you can't remember the last time you engaged in your hobby.

- You usually feel exhausted for no particular reason.

- You're always intending to exercise, but you never seem to be able to work it into your schedule.

- You go to work when you're sick.

- You have very few close relationships beyond your immediate family.

- Your partner or child is often annoyed by your relationship with your device.

Burnout: When Well-Being Is Ignored

In addition to the personal and day-to-day organizational costs of not attending to the human side of human capital (namely the well-being of yourself and your staff), the long-term effect is burnout, which can strike any employee and is always disappointing, but it is particularly calamitous to the organization when it happens to a key employee. Burnout is more intense than stress, and often the results are more dire. According to psychiatrist Dr. Harry Levinson, the symptoms of burnout include chronic fatigue, anger at those making demands, self-criticism for putting up with the demands, cynicism, negativity, irritability, a sense of being besieged, and hair-trigger display of emotions.[24] Burnout often leads to extreme situations like hospitalization, drug or alcohol abuse, and divorce.

The potential for burnout is one reason to pay attention to long work hours and lack of balance in your employees. Other causes that leadership can affect include job monotony, the perception of little or no control over work, and the attempt to be everything to everyone.

Institutional Changes: Programs to Make Your Employees' Lives Easier

Attending to the issues discussed in this chapter is part of being a good leader of knowledge workers. Supporting the well-being of your team is not only good for business; it's also the right thing to do. As Clayton Christensen says in his blockbuster essay for the *Harvard Business Review*:

> Management is the most noble of professions if it's practiced well. No other occupation offers as many ways to help others learn and grow, take responsibility and be recognized for achievement, and contribute to the success of a team.[25]

In addition to getting intentional about the issues discussed earlier, there are also corporate initiatives that you can implement to instill the value of caring for employees' well-being, individually and as corporate assets, into the day-to-day operations of the organization. The following list addresses several, and you will find additional suggestions and recommendations in every chapter of this book:

1. **New training:** It's time to update traditional training agendas! Workflow-management training from the perspective of attention management, rather than time management, is a necessary addition to corporate development initiatives for knowledge workers. Mindfulness training is a powerful complement to work-life-management training.

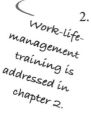

Work-life-management training is addressed in chapter 2.

2. **Support staff:** Gone are the days when all executives had a personal secretary, but I think it's time to revisit the lessons of those days. The reason they're gone may be the assumption that technology exists that can handle the administrative tasks once done by executive assistants, office managers, and other clerical staff, but the truth is that the job of finding and learning that technology is often a barrier to using it, and there is still much that technology can't do.

The purpose of support staff is to offload lower-skill and non-specialty tasks to lower-paid employees, so that higher-paid staff can spend more time adding value (the unique and highly specialized skills and talents for which they were hired) commensurate with their salary. In addition to the benefits of lightening the load for your executives and other specialized staff, the math makes sense.

Support Staff Improves Your Bottom Line

For example, let's say you have four sales executives, each bringing in $200,000 per year in revenue. If you could offload some of their administrative tasks such that they increased their revenue just 5 percent annually, you could offset the cost of a full-time administrative person for at least $30,000 per year plus benefits. Any amount of improvement over that 5 percent gain goes directly to the bottom line, and studies indicate that the odds are in your favor.[26]

There's a second benefit that is hard to quantify but easy to understand in this distraction-rich business environment. According to Melba Duncan writing in the *Harvard Business Review*, "A good assistant can filter the distractions that can turn a manager into a reactive type who spends all day answering email instead of a leader who proactively sets the organization's agenda."[27]

While business has moved away from this support-staff model, other industries, such as the medical field, have embraced it. It's unlikely you'll find a licensed medical doctor, who makes six figures annually, taking blood or administering flu shots that a technician can be paid to do for much less. The most productive people know that the most important questions are "Can someone else do this for me?" and "How else could this get done?"

What Can Your Team Delegate?

The self-assessment from *Harvard Business Review*, found at https://hbr.org/web/2013/08/assessment/make-time-for-work-that-matters, can help your team quickly identify tasks that can be outsourced. Another exercise is to have your executives start a list of "items to delegate." After a week or two, the length of that list can be a good indicator of the need for support staff or a good foundation for a discussion about it.

3. **Outsourced assistance:** If increasing headcount with administrative staff is not feasible for your organization, consider an outsourced model. Facilitate employees' ability to take advantage of the "access economy" (also known as platform business models), which are companies that provide "tasks as a service."[28] Some examples are businesses that provide errand-running, personal administration, household chores, meal delivery or meal planning service, and home repair and maintenance services. (Appendix A contains a partial but extensive list of these businesses.)

Support your employees in taking advantage of these services that make their lives easier by creating corporate relationships, negotiating discounts, offering gift cards, and even including a stipend in compensation packages. In addition to national companies, you can also facilitate relationships with local businesses, such as by becoming a pick-up/drop-off location for dry cleaning services and grocery-delivery services, and/or maintain a list of vetted babysitters and handyman providers. These services are not only useful in supporting your staff's personal lives, but also in many cases they can be used as an alternative to hiring administrative support staff. For example, if your sales team doesn't have an administrator, offering a stipend to hire a virtual assistant for travel booking, expense report filing, appointment setting, and other administrative tasks can make life easier for your sales staff, and it can remove some of the monotony from their work and free them to spend more time on the work they enjoy.

4. **Corporate mentoring programs:** For new hires, high-potential employees, and anyone who could benefit from some professional

guidance, a corporate mentoring program could be the perfect solution. Mentoring can assist with work-life balance challenges, employee engagement, and knowledge transfer and succession planning, among other things. The program can be formal or informal, but it should be voluntary on the part of both the mentor and the mentee. The Forrester Report "Drive Employee Talent Development Through Business Mentoring Programs" includes these other factors for a successful program: [29]

- Structured with organized mentor/mentee profiles
- Includes training on mentoring best practices and instruction on using mentoring software
- Requires a commitment from the mentoring pair to work together for a period of time, usually up to a year
- Can include some mentors working with more than one employee and mentors may also be mentees themselves
- Permits mentor/mentee partnerships that exist across lines of business and even across geographies

Mentoring has even more benefits for companies with remote staff, because it can help keep them engaged and retained.

Adjusting your training plans, taking another look at administrative support, and implementing formal or informal corporate mentoring programs are only changes that can be made at the leadership level. But they will all help convey the message that you care about your employees as individuals. This is the sign of a good leader and can go a long way toward improving the culture at your organization.

- -

Conclusion

Intentional and formalized consideration of employees' physical, mental, and emotional wellness, and particularly filling the gap of "holistic well-being" left by engagement and wellness programs, are important factors of success for leaders of knowledge workers. Leaders, too, are knowledge workers, and have the same needs. The complete formula includes small, day-to-day changes in operations, leadership commitment and modeling, plus larger, strategic and institutional initiatives. But even small steps in the right direction can offer significant payoff to organizations. You can help, whether you have the authority at your organization to institute all the changes, some of the changes, or even if you just voice suggestions or model the behaviors in an effort to influence others. Studies show that what leaders say is far less important than what they do.[30]

📋 Action Items

These are specific steps that will help you put the information in this chapter to use immediately. Most can be implemented relatively quickly and easily and can pay big returns:

1. Assess your office kitchen: Do you offer snacks? If not, consider adding some healthy options to your supply order. If you do, ensure they are foods that power optimal brain functioning and will keep your team energized throughout the day.

2. Support napping at work: Encourage employees to take short naps to recharge. If possible, set aside a quiet space for napping by investing in an "energy pod" or a couch in a room that has some extra space. Purchase a room divider if you can't dedicate a whole room. Purchasing an inexpensive white noise machine with a timer/alarm would be an added bonus.

3. Update your training agenda: Training in mindfulness and attention management will improve your team's mental well-being.

4. Add support staff or provide a stipend for outsourced solutions: When your knowledge workers can delegate routine and administrative tasks, they have more time for the work that's most satisfying to them—and valuable to you.

5. Support personal outsourcing: Start by asking your employees about their favorite dry cleaner and become a pick-up/drop-off location. Assemble a team to propose other innovative ideas to

www.attentionmanagement.com

make it easy for your team members to take advantage of services that help them take personal tasks like meal planning and home maintenance off their plates.

6. Include work-life balance as a mentoring topic: If you already have a mentoring program in place or you are starting a new program, make work-life balance one of the topics covered.

💬 Takeaways You Can Tweet

Here are important points of the chapter summarized so that they are easy to digest, but also so that you can conveniently share the information with your followers on Twitter or on other social media outlets. Follow and participate in the conversation online using *#workwithout-walls*, and/or my handle, @mnthomas.

- ❏ In a knowledge economy, brainpower is the most valuable resource. So improving productivity means maximizing yours.
- ❏ The three mental states that drive performance are calm, happy, and energized. https://hbr.org/2014/12/how-your-state-of-mind-affects-your-performance
- ❏ Engagement and wellness programs are great, but they leave a hole with regard to optimal mental states that drive performance.
- ❏ Cutting sugar and carbs and providing energy-sustaining food at meetings and in break room will boost your team's productivity.
- ❏ When you encourage napping at work, you encourage productivity.
- ❏ We crave control over work, but traditional time management training doesn't teach it. New work requires new rules.
- ❏ Learning mindfulness offers an optimal state of mind for productivity, plus increases work satisfaction and performance.

❏ Our brains need work-life balance for improved creativity, motivation, and productivity.

❏ You might be surprised to see how much you can add to your bottom line by hiring support for your team.

❏ Making it easy for your team to use services that let them outsource chores and tasks will increase their productivity.

❏ Implement a mentoring program at your company and make work-life balance a focus.

Chapter 2

DISTRACTION, ATTENTION, AND THE TWENTY-FIRST CENTURY WORK CULTURE

What information consumes is rather obvious. It consumes the attention of its recipients. Hence a wealth of information creates a poverty of attention.[31]

—HERBERT A. SIMON, NOBEL PRIZE-WINNING ECONOMIST

So many walls are falling in today's world of work. New technologies mean that work distracts us while we're at home or anywhere, and online socializing, entertainment, and other personal pursuits tempt us at the office. Advances in technology also mean that, for better or for worse, we can work any time because the office can travel with us wherever we go. At our offices, even physical walls are falling—open offices are on the rise; private offices seem like a relic of the 1950s.

Work without walls can cause an environment that is frantic and immediate, and requires technology use that erodes our attention span and lures us to constantly multitask. This chapter addresses each of these issues in detail.

Distraction Sabotages Knowledge Work

Today's rapidly changing technological landscape has come with a requirement that knowledge workers successfully manage a tidal wave of information and interruptions.

This new world of work without walls presents opportunities, but it also illuminates the problem that most workplaces aren't adequately addressing: distraction. It affects all levels within the workforce, including leadership. It has corporate culture firmly in its grip, and it wreaks havoc in many organizations.

Distraction is insidious not only in its professional consequences but also in its personal consequences. Distraction deprives our brains of the rest and renewal we need to cultivate creativity and fresh insights. Knowledge workers—whose products are information, communication, and complex decision-making—are particularly susceptible to the harm caused by distraction.[32]

Distraction is one of the most important, yet least recognized, issues of the changing work environment.

We are distracted from our lives at home and on vacation by the intrusion of work-related communication that's ever-present on our mobile devices. And when we're at work, we're distracted from our work and from thinking, absorbing, and applying information in a meaningful way by the noise of a group setting, the technology we use, and the ways in which we use that technology. Off-site work does not make us immune to these distractions; technology is never far from reach, which means that entertainment and personal matters beckon, regardless of our location.

Old-fashioned time management isn't up to the challenge of helping employees regain control over their attention. It's time to discard old techniques and behaviors that were created in a world without the Internet, smartphones, and wearable technology. Those hard-to-ignore demands tempt us and stealthily erode our ability to control our own attention, and hence our time, since how we manage our time is only relevant to the extent that we also devote our *attention* to the task at hand.

We often give our time to a task, but during that time, only give it our attention intermittently, in small increments, as we switch between the task and the constant interruptions: email, text messages, instant messages, our own thoughts, and other

> **How we manage our time is only relevant to the extent that we also devote our attention to the task at hand.**

people. The result is that despite the time commitment, the outcome is a very different experience from the one that we intended. Research shows that when we are task-switching, we make much less progress than expected. Instead of time management, your focus should be on a more relevant twenty-first-century concept—attention management—as the antidote to distraction.

Why Are We So Distracted?

In the past, people worked when they were at the office, and for most, it was relatively easy to disconnect after hours. Rapid technological advances and digital convergence have changed all that. The number and type of communication tools to which we have access has exploded: email, instant messages, text messages, and myriad social media channels. Things that used to be separate—TV, books, communication channels, newspapers, etc.—have now converged into one portable device. This is known as digital convergence. Mobile devices have become ubiquitous in our lives, and they are also great delivery mechanisms for the very foundation of knowledge work—information and communication. Yet constantly having a screen in front of us, whether it is a smartphone, tablet, laptop, navigation system, or television, creates an unrelenting stream of potential distraction.

On top of the technological distractions, workers must also deal with the distracting nature of the modern work environment. Various reports say that approximately 70 percent of workplaces use an open-office floor plan. Research has shown that employees in open offices experience reduced attention spans, productivity, creative thinking, concentration, and motivation.[33] Many workers prefer to work full-time or part-time at home instead of in an office, but remote work has its own set of challenges.

Open-office floor plans are addressed in Chapter 5. Remote work and telecommuting are addressed in Chapter 6.

Digital Convergence Poses a Problem

Digital convergence refers to the merging of previously distinct information channels into a single technology—namely, the ability to use a single device to watch television and movies; read books, magazines, and newspapers; socialize; work; play games; book travel; and participate in a host of other activities (including those we don't necessarily intend, such as watching videos of animals and babies). This technology often has the ability to "push" constant indicators and notifications, tempting users to continually engage and inadvertently allow their attention to be stolen.

Generational Issues Are Less Relevant

While "managing millennials" is a hot topic in the media, and many experts have devoted their careers to educating business owners on this topic, research summarized in the *Harvard Business Review* shows no compelling evidence to support generational stereotypes, so making management decisions based on supposed stereotypes is problematic.[34] What is different is that never before have we had such a large population from so many different generations all working together. This does call for special attention to tensions among age groups, especially with regard to technology and communication preferences. In my experience, millennials in general seem to prefer written communication via technology, and they have high expectations for fast responses.

Millennials are also more prone to multitasking and have less patience for doing only one thing at a time. And it's true that a twenty-something is better at this than a fifty-something, but in general most people don't do it well.

I've found in my work that older professionals are more apt to prioritize other work over email and other written communication, and they have less demanding expectations for response times. They also tend to have more patience and longer attention spans, and therefore older professionals find it somewhat easier to single-task, especially when they learn how much more efficient it is.

In these ways and others, boomers and millennials "speak different languages," but these are simply interpersonal issues not unlike any other mismatch of relational styles. It's similar to how some people are big-picture thinkers, so they have less patience for detail-oriented discussions. There are many ways people are different, and age is one that has always been present in the workplace.

Wearable Technology Is an Increasing Concern

Wearable technology is one preference that is more common to the younger generations, and it's expected to become more prevalent over the next few years. This will only increase opportunities for distraction. The business value (or detriment) of wearable technology is yet to be determined, but the expectation is that more and more workers will be wearing connected devices.

Trapped in Reactivity

The problem's not just that we're getting distracted from work; it's also that we're getting distracted from important work by *other work*. How many times have you sat down to do thoughtful, in-depth tasks, only to be lured away by incoming emails from clients or colleagues? Faced with the flood of incoming information, interruptions, and distractions, many knowledge workers are so overwhelmed that they spend much of their time "playing defense," are less able to identify priorities, and stay mostly in reactive mode. Work comes at them from half a dozen places all at once, so they get quickly overwhelmed trying to remember and manage it.

The pace is frantic, with a new interruption every few minutes, so it feels like there is no time to stop and organize it all. In fact, workers are distracted so often that in the increasingly rare absence of constant distraction, they find themselves bored, and they seek out distraction! The environment chips away at their attention span until they rarely or never have the patience to do only one thing at a time, so they constantly check email, instant messages, social media pages, etc., to pounce on anything that seems to need a response, providing convenient justification for their need for distraction.

Additionally, these communication channels often bring new tasks and details at a fast and frantic pace, so workers often operate without a clear picture of their total

> *It's easy for knowledge workers to confuse being busy with being productive.*

responsibilities. Instead, they flit between email, voicemail, meeting notes, and their various haphazard to-do lists to try to keep track of priorities. Since most workers have no clear plan, it's faster and easier to spend the majority of their time reacting to what happens to them rather than proactively tracking and acting upon the most important or the highest-impact activities. It's easy for knowledge workers to confuse being busy with being productive when faced with this combination of the

- ➤ Frantic pace
- ➤ Constant distractions
- ➤ Urge to multitask
- ➤ Lack of a clear picture of their responsibilities
- ➤ Plethora of incoming communication channels.

Indeed, when employees are constantly task-switching, productivity suffers. Studies show that multitasking causes tasks to take longer, and it causes the quality of the results to be lower. Constant multitasking makes us more prone to making mistakes, more likely to miss important information and cues, and less likely to retain information in working memory, which impairs problem solving and creativity.[35]

Constant reactivity also deprives employees of the quiet, uninterrupted time they need to do their most meaningful work and even of the pauses they need to recharge their brains. People need what neuroscientists call *controlled attention* to do thoughtful work such as writing, planning, creating, and strategizing. We also need the pauses, when there isn't too much stimulus and we aren't trying to focus on anything in particular. This is *restorative attention*, and it's the quiet times that our brains need to process information. It's often when insights are generated.

For knowledge workers, downtime is key, both away from the office, but also at work, in the form of breaks and the space to be reflective and thoughtfully proactive. Since the product of knowledge work is the creation, distribution, or application of knowledge, their work benefits from a fresh perspective, which can't be achieved if employees never fully disconnect from work.[36] Knowledge work also benefits from continual learning, which is impeded by constant distraction. Learning occurs only when information gets absorbed in a focused and meaningful way. You hired your knowledge workers for the edge their wisdom, experience, and ability to learn would give your business, not for how many tasks they can seemingly do at once or how many emails they can answer in a day. Use the ideas in the "Institutional Changes" and "Action Items" sections of this chapter to ensure that you and your leadership team are creating an office environment and company culture that supports the appropriate balance of downtime; thinking time; and productive, proactive time.

A culture that supports single-tasking and focus helps employees feel less scattered and distracted and therefore less stressed, contributing to their feeling of well-being at work and, ultimately, to their productivity.

Distraction Interferes with Customer Service

Is your customer support or technical support staff responsible for both receiving the customer issues and resolving the customer issues? If so, they won't be able to bring their full attention to solving the problem if they can't take a break from receiving more problems! Consider organizing the days of your support staff so that each staffer has time away from phone and email. Another option would be to appoint a "triage" person who handles intake only and then assigns the problems to others for solutions. Either of these will provide an opportunity for support staff to devote their full attention to solving problems. This will likely result in happier customers, and, when staff has an opportunity to really reflect on issues, they are better primed to recognize systemic problems and opportunities for product and policy improvements. Train your staff that good customer service means not only responding to customers in a timely manner but also solving their problems in a thorough, attentive, and satisfactory way. Then use the ideas from *Work Without Walls* to create an environment that supports this training.

Time-Management Training Doesn't Work

While work has changed, the training we get about how to organize and manage our work (time management) looks pretty much the same as it always has. Traditional time management teaches us to:

- > **Start every morning making a list of things to do that day.** But once we check our email, that list is already woefully outdated.
- > **Prioritize A, B, and C.** But these days, everything seems urgent and competes for the highest priority.
- > **Close the door to get important work done.** But this doesn't address our spinning brains and the lure of the Internet at our fingertips (let alone the fact that, in many cases, we no longer have a door).

➤ **Schedule important tasks on your calendar.** But whatever "schedule" we came up with is typically out the window by 8:01 a.m.

Work-life-management skills are not taught in school, and as a result, workers are often left to their own devices (sticky notes, flags in email, writing and reviewing paper lists, etc.) with mixed results. There are too many sticky notes, the paper lists are way too long and scattered and there's always more to add to them, and flagged emails quickly fall below the scroll and get buried. Email is a struggle because it's essentially an endless list of tasks to manage, and most people don't have a good process for managing tasks.

These skills (such as they are) vary across the workplace and make it difficult to track overall work and progress, which leaves company productivity to chance.

Institutional Changes: Provide Comprehensive Productivity Training

The truth is, we have to work differently now, and we need a new kind of training to be truly effective. Traditional time-management principles don't address today's level of distraction. Innovative, forward-thinking leadership should offer comprehensive productivity training as a replacement

> **For knowledge workers, peak productivity means having clarity over goals and expectations, a workflow-management system to meet them, and control over distractions and attention.**

for its outdated training predecessor—time-management training. This instruction would include:

➤ **Clarity from leadership regarding expectations:** Specifically, expectations about:
  - Workers' availability
  - Output and outcomes
➤ **Attention management:** Teaching staff how to reverse the trend of constant distraction, maintain their focus for

longer periods of time, single-task for faster and higher-quality results, and be more present in both their personal life and their professional life.

➤ **Work-life-management:** Offering a detailed and thorough process for effectively handling all the details of life and work, including commitments, responsibilities, communication, and information.

Comprehensive productivity training can provide a significant return on investment and empower employees to overcome these new challenges. Anecdotally, my clients tell me they regain an hour or more of productive time per day. This could make a difference at an organization equivalent to one or more additional full-time staffers. In addition, of my clients who report in up to ninety days after attending training, more than 97 percent say they feel more productive, and 95 percent report that they feel more in control over work and life. This contributes to reduced turnover and absenteeism, so the further savings from hiring, training, and lost workdays is exponential.

Clarity from Leadership

The first component in the success of this training is clarity from leadership regarding expectations about workers' availability, and output and outcomes. I believe that the most important measurement of knowledge work is related to the more qualitative factors of employee engagement and their attitudes about their work. And clear communication about expectations of availability is necessary for knowledge workers to achieve balance. These issues are addressed fully in chapters 1 and 3.

However, knowledge work can also be measured in terms of output and outcomes, and these measurement factors should be devised in conjunction with the worker. This measurement concept is discussed in detail in chapter 7.

Implementing the ideas in these chapters provides the clarity necessary to impact:

➤ Workers' work-life balance

➤ How they feel about their job

➤ The measurement of output and outcomes

The other components of comprehensive productivity training are attention-management skills and a good workflow-management system.

Attention Management

Productivity training must be reframed from the old ideas of time management, which are no longer relevant. Attention-management skills provide employees with control over their work, thus avoiding the internal distractions created when responsibilities and tasks aren't well tracked and organized. Studies show that control makes people happy, and happy people are more productive employees.[37] Attention-management training teaches employees the ability to control distractions—both internal distractions from a spinning brain and external distractions caused by technology and other people—to single-task for higher-quality results, and to engage in sustained (controlled) attention when necessary, which should be a part of almost every day. Education and awareness are big parts of this training. For example, staff should be taught that while it may seem that multitasking helps us get more done, the research shows otherwise.[38] And calling attention to unproductive behaviors, such as being constantly reactive rather than thoughtfully proactive, helps employees (and leadership) recognize when they are engaging in these behaviors.

An environment that is set up to support focus and value single-tasking also prevents bad habits from taking root. These practices, especially when modeled by leadership, protect a company, and its employees, against an unhealthy and distracted corporate culture.

Workflow Management

In a good workflow-management system, major goals, restated as projects, are always visible and available, as are the specific actions needed to achieve them. These serve as an anchor in a sea of distraction. Many employees track the majority of their workload (and their "life load") in their heads, causing them to be distracted with the burden of remembering. But you can only truly manage what you can see, and you can only see what is outside your head, where it becomes tangible, centralized, actionable, and trackable.

An effective workflow-management process (such as my Empowered Productivity System[39]) helps employees combat distractions—especially the internal distractions caused by mentally running down a to-do list all day, trying to ensure nothing is forgotten. It also makes tasks and responsibilities easy to organize, track, and act upon, further quieting that spinning brain. In addition to the individual productivity benefits, making staff workloads more tangible offers further benefits to the organization:

> *You can only truly manage what you can see, and you can only see what is outside your head, where it becomes tangible, centralized, actionable, and trackable.*

- ➤ Workloads, including output and outcomes, are more easily quantifiable, which assists in human resource allocation.
- ➤ Appropriate resource allocation provides insight into turnover problems.
- ➤ Employee reviews and merit rewards are more objective.
- ➤ Job descriptions can be more accurate, leading to better hiring.
- ➤ Institutional knowledge and company history is documented.
- ➤ Accountability is enhanced.
- ➤ Lack of progress due to inadequate understanding or skills becomes easier to identify.
- ➤ Project timelines are more accurate, and bottlenecks can be anticipated.
- ➤ Accomplishments become apparent, which is important because progress is a powerful motivator.
- ➤ Low performers are less able to conceal their lack of progress.
- ➤ Responsibilities can be more easily absorbed in the event of a prolonged absence or departure.

Being our most productive and effective in an information-rich, ever-changing workplace isn't instinctual. But it can be learned if outdated concepts like time management are tossed aside for more modern ideas on productivity. Comprehensive productivity training requires clarity from leadership on employees' work, and incorporates attention management and workflow management to help employees regain control.

Conclusion

The challenges to making institutional changes are many, but the good news is that human beings have an impressive capacity to adapt. We'll never adapt as fast as technology advances, but we can learn to acclimate to our ever-evolving environment. What's necessary is the recognition of the behaviors that are sabotaging our productivity, attention, and brainpower. When we recognize that we are training ourselves to be distracted, we can reverse the detrimental effects. Focus, or our ability to control our attention, is a skill like any other, and with practice it gets stronger. Business leaders can offer these new comprehensive productivity skills to employees and create office environments and culture that bring out the best in their staff.

Action Items

These are specific steps that will help you put the information in this chapter to use immediately. Most can be implemented relatively quickly and easily and can pay big returns:

1. Add to your staff development plans comprehensive productivity training that helps leaders gain clarity over expectations and that includes both attention management and a comprehensive workflow-management system.

2. In a leadership meeting, make a list of attributes of an office environment that supports downtime; thinking time; and productive, proactive time. Make a plan to implement these

attributes, vocally advocate for them, and discourage any behaviors that work against this environment.

3. Meet with your customer service staff to find ways for them to work with fewer distractions. Some ideas: Give each staffer time away from phone and email, appoint one team member to handle intake and assign problems to others for solutions. Emphasize to staff that good customer service is not just timely; it's also thorough and attentive.

4. Have a leadership meeting with the express goal to clarify and communicate your expectations about workers' availability and how you will measure success.

5. In words and behavior, send a message that single-tasking is more effective than multitasking. Give your employees your full attention in meetings and when speaking one-on-one.

6. Help your employees recognize when they're engaging in unproductive behaviors, such as being constantly reactive rather than thoughtfully proactive.

🗩 Takeaways You Can Tweet

Here are important points of the chapter summarized so that they are easy to digest, but also so that you can conveniently share the information with your followers on Twitter or on other social media outlets. Follow and participate in the conversation online using *#workwithoutwalls,* and/or my handle, @mnthomas.

❑ Distraction is one of the most important & least recognized issues of the changing work environment.

❑ Distraction is insidious in both professional & personal consequences.

❑ Traditional time-management training doesn't give employees the tools they need to deal with constant distraction.

- ❑ It's easy for knowledge workers to confuse being busy with being productive.

- ❑ Studies show that multitasking causes tasks to take longer & the quality of the results to be lower.

- ❑ Traditional time-management principles don't help much because they don't sufficiently address distraction.

- ❑ Operating in peak productivity means having good attention management skills, specific goals, and a reliable work-life-management system.

- ❑ Attention management skills provide employees with control over their work.

Chapter 3

THE CHALLENGE OF EMAIL AND THE DANGERS OF CONSTANT COMMUNICATION

If conventional wisdom now says that constant work is necessary for professional success, I can't think of a more important time to buck convention.[40]

—MAURA NEVEL THOMAS

PERHAPS nothing is more emblematic of the idea of work without walls than email. Thanks to our portable devices, email can find us anywhere, any time. It breaks down the walls between work and personal time. It also can penetrate the walls we try to put up to protect the time we need for our important work.

Email and other communications tools are supposed to boost productivity, but they often end up sabotaging it. As with most productivity issues, this problem is less an issue of the tool itself, and more an issue of the beliefs, perspectives, practices, and behaviors of the users. If your employees are trapped in their inboxes, it's time for a culture change.

Shift Your Perspective on Email

The ability to "manage" email is either the holy grail of office productivity or the bane of the knowledge workers' existence. Key phrases related to "managing email" have hundreds of millions of searches on Google daily. Endless articles have been written, and there is a plethora of tools, apps, games, and techniques that exist to purportedly teach knowledge workers how to deal effectively with email. Employees struggle, and corporate cultural norms perpetuate the struggle.

In my work, I see frantic and stressful corporate cultures created by the pace of today's communication tools. While at work, most people keep their email/instant message/social media pages open and downloading all day, so they can respond immediately to any communication. This habit can be driven by several factors—including boredom, procrastination, poor productivity skills, or the desire to be seen as particularly responsive. And yet my clients tell me, "I would get so much done if only I didn't have email." What this sentiment and this practice tell me is that the way people view email needs to change. Those clients perhaps would get more done, but eventually they would run out of work for the simple reason that, for better or for worse, most knowledge workers receive the majority of their daily tasks, from both internal and external sources, via email. This means email isn't something to squeeze in around your "real work." Email *is* real work, too, and therefore it requires real, dedicated time.

The "Skim and Skip" Trap

The behaviors I see most people exhibit when dealing with email is what I call "skim and skip." As each message comes in, they quickly skim it, unconsciously evaluating it against two criteria: (1) Is it urgent? (2) Can I quickly dispatch it? (Meaning delete, file, or answer.) You may recognize this behavior in yourself. I can virtually guarantee you will witness this behavior in your employees. It's very common.

Many busy knowledge workers schedule their days heavily and somehow think that they'll stay on top of email in the brief gaps between meetings and "real work." However, during that "real work," they multi-task by jumping between email and other work. We can hardly blame the employee; this behavior was born of an environment where any message could be a mundane, system-generated notification or an urgent and critical issue from the boss or the most important client. Email brings it all, and everything in between, so employees frantically skim every message as it lands in their inbox, inspired by the constant fear that they will miss something important. As the message count keeps spiraling, email bleeds into their personal time. They try to catch up in line at the grocery store, at the family dinner table, or while watching TV.

People who treat email this way tend to get caught in "skim and skip" mode. Because they don't allow time to really deal with (what I call "processing") their email in a more thoughtful way, they scan for messages that seem easy, exciting, or critical to deal with, leaving anything that seems more complicated until later.

"Later" Never Comes

When your team members use the skim and skip method of dealing with email, they are setting themselves up for problems:

- ➤ That mythical "later" never seems to come, which means that important matters in the emails they've been skipping fall by the wayside.
- ➤ Those skipped messages still weigh on them—especially when they are flagged or marked as unread—and increase stress.
- ➤ They likely read those lingering messages repeatedly without acting on them, meaning they work less efficiently.
- ➤ When email creeps into any pocket of time that appears during the day, the opportunity for beneficial, restorative breaks are lost.
- ➤ When constantly switching to email while doing other tasks, the quality of both the original task and the processing of the email suffer.

The solution to effectively managing email requires changes in both the individual and the organization.

The Individual Solution

First, and most importantly, all people in the organization need to change the way they view email. This idea that it's something to be squeezed in between "real work" is a fantasy; email is work! Individuals must acknowledge that email is *real* work that deserves *real* time and attention.

> *Daydreaming in the grocery line can actually be more productive than checking email. Seemingly idle times like that are often the very moments when we have mental breakthroughs.*[41]

Of course, not *all* email can be classified as real work. We all get newsletters and other mail that we want (but don't necessarily need in the middle of our workday), plus spam, junk, and system-generated messages we don't read, and we should make every effort to manage and minimize those types of messages (more on that later in this chapter). But the rest of the messages, probably the majority of the messages, are actual work, from both internal and external customers.

Be Realistic

Encourage your team members to be realistic about how much time it will take to manage, organize, and process the work they receive via email, and model this behavior yourself. Use this as a starting point: My experience shows that the average professional gets about one hundred messages per day, and each message takes an average of two minutes to process. That's two hundred minutes—three hours and twenty minutes—of email (otherwise known as WORK) to do *every day*. On a day full of meetings, when there is no time to dedicate to messages, it's safe to assume that more than six hours of work will be waiting for you in your email inbox the following day. The realistic thing to do is to plan accordingly, yet most people leave *no* time in their schedule to deal with this work.

Compounding this problem is that I see many of my knowledge worker clients spending spend three to five, or more, hours in meetings *every day*. We think of employees as having an eight- or nine-hour workday, so four or more hours of meetings seems realistic. But it's time to face the reality that this is only true if attending meetings is basically *the only task* your employees have. Add the average three hours and twenty minutes of email to a day with four hours of meetings, and that gives you a workday of seven-plus hours, before factoring in any time to stop and think, eat, rest, speak to anyone else, **do any other tasks,** or use the bathroom! If your employees get invited to meetings for twenty (or more) hours per week, they may feel backed into a corner. Have you considered, and communicated, what you expect your employees to do in that situation? (See Figure 3.1.)

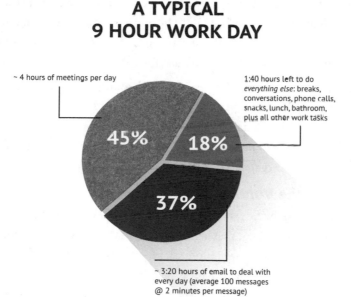

A TYPICAL
9 HOUR WORK DAY

~ 4 hours of meetings per day

1:40 hours left to do *everything else*: breaks, conversations, phone calls, snacks, lunch, bathroom, plus all other work tasks

45% **18%**

37%

~ 3:20 hours of email to deal with every day (average 100 messages @ 2 minutes per message)

Figure 3.1. *Unrealistic Workday.*

Tech-Free Meetings Are More Effective

Encourage employees to come to meetings without their technology, and/or keep a basket or box in meeting areas to store electronics until the end of the meeting. If participants object to having technology-free meetings because they want to type notes, you can share with them that studies show that handwriting notes supports learning in a way that typing notes does not.[42] There are at least two reasons for this.

First, there is a hand-brain connection that occurs when we write but is absent when we type. Also, most people type very fast, often fast enough to capture a thought verbatim from the speaker. Handwriting is slower, so it causes people to assimilate the information when they paraphrase and abbreviate the ideas to capture them in writing.

As the leader, also ask yourself this: Does *your* schedule include sufficient time every day to deal with all the messages that come to you via email, or do you feel that you are behind on your messages? If you don't allow sufficient time, why not? If it's because the messages that come to you via email are mostly unimportant, then you should consider ways to more effectively manage these messages.

Encourage your employees to start leaving more room on their calendars. They need some unscheduled time not only for email but also for proactive work. You may need to help them prioritize the meetings they need to attend, and you may also need to examine the meeting practices at your organization.

Minimize the Volume

One way to stem the flow is to use the rules or filter feature of your email client so that non-urgent messages, such as newsletters and system-generated messages, are either automatically deleted or automatically sent to a folder. Make sure that the messages are labeled as "read" so that the folders don't add to your stress by showing numerous unread messages.

Read my review of Throttle at http://regainyourtime.com/email-management-tool-review-throttle/.

Also be sure you are taking advantage of the "junk" feature of your email client, and you can even consider adding another spam/message filtering service. I've found SpamDrain (www.spamdrain.com) to be an indispensable service for this purpose. You can also use a service to bundle non-urgent emails, such as professional newsletters, into a daily digest that you can read at your convenience. My favorite service is Throttle (www.throttle.com). A third option is to unsubscribe from messages you no longer want. There are services that will do this for you, such as Unroll.me (www.unroll.me).

If your staff copies you on lots of messages that you don't read, either discuss this with your team or automatically divert those messages to a folder and have them marked as read using rules in your email client. Employing these techniques will minimize the amount of email you receive and ensure that the messages that land in your inbox are necessary messages about real work from real people.

Use a Process for Managing Email

The following suggestions will help you support your team members in managing their email—and will also help you manage your own email:

> **Review messages as often as you feel that you need to.** By *review* I mean just skim your inbox for messages that are urgent or can be quickly handled. Do this *in between* other tasks—not during them. This single-tasking, rather than constant task-switching or multitasking, will ensure that your tasks will be done faster and better. When "reviewing" email, do this only on a handheld device because you're less likely to get permanently distracted on your device (because it's too small) than you would be on your computer.

> *Chapters 11 and 12 of **Personal Productivity Secrets** (my first book) outlines a more comprehensive process for managing email, and chapter 15 of that book is full of techniques for making meetings more efficient.*

> **Decide how often you should set aside time to** *process* **email**, which means thoughtfully reading each message and handling everything you can, or adding items from email to a task list to handle at an appropriate later time. The goal during processing is to empty your inbox. I suggest processing your inbox down to zero at least a couple of times per week and doing your processing on your computer, as opposed to a portable device. Your computer's operating system has all the "bells and whistles" that make it easier

to deal with messages, such as the ability to easily transfer information to another program, or to easily create a task from an email. As of this writing, the abbreviated operating systems on most portable devices don't have everything you need to process email efficiently.

How Much Time for Processing?

How often you need to process your email depends on your role. I find that the expectations for CEOs and senior leadership are a bit less demanding than for others in the organization. It's typical for senior leadership to be a bit less "available." If you have a customer-facing role, or you work in a support position, you'll likely need to process messages more often. Only you can decide what seems right given your role. If you feel that you need to answer email immediately, it might be because you've set the expectation that you answer messages immediately. If you reset that expectation, eventually the people you interact with will come to understand your new behaviors. Remember: email was never intended to be a synchronous (real-time) communication tool. For all but the most time-sensitive positions, like IT support, I have found anywhere from four to eight business hours to be a reasonable response time. You may have to review email more often than once or twice per day just due to the sheer volume. Give this some deliberate thought and make a conscious decision about both how often you will review email, and how much time in your day you will leave available for email processing.

Whatever schedule you create for processing your email, give it your full thought and attention when that time comes:

> ➤ **Read each message fully; don't just skim it.** Act on it if you can dispatch it in a few minutes or less. Otherwise, add it to your task list.

> ➤ **Stop the download of new incoming messages while you're working to clear your current messages.** Work in offline mode while you're processing your messages; otherwise, you'll find you won't get very far. Every time you deal with one message, one or more new messages will come in. This would be like trying to dig a hole while someone stands beside you and throws the dirt back in!

It might sound paradoxical, but when you start treating email as real work, you'll find that it takes less time and that it's no longer a constant source of stress and anxiety.

The Organizational Solution

Besides improving employees' personal habits, you should also look at your workplace culture regarding email. This includes habits exhibited by leadership, corporate systems, and company hardware. Do your company practices and expectations support efficient, balanced, and productive use of email? Or have habits and assumptions taken root to sabotage your employees' energy, effectiveness, and efficiency?

Stop Crowding Out True Productivity

If you always expect an immediate response to your emails, you have (perhaps inadvertently) tied your employees to their inboxes. Even if you don't expect an immediate response, do your employees think you do? Or do they think you will look more favorably on an immediate response? When companies fall into the habit of using internal email for immediate and urgent communication, the (often unintended) byproduct is that employees are forced to always leave their email open, so they're distracted by every new message that comes in.

Having such a culture of immediate response puts employees in reactive mode all day and prevents them from being proactive. They aren't assessing their *A reactive work culture means important work takes a backseat to immediate demands.* overall workload and choosing what to work on next. Important work takes a backseat to immediate demands. This kind of email culture also creates constant multitasking (task-switching) and prevents employees from ever being able to focus on the task at hand for any period of time. Study after study shows that task-switching causes work to both take longer and be of lower quality.[43] I often hear from clients that they find it difficult even to begin a larger task because they anticipate interruptions and, therefore, feel discouraged to even get started.

Manage Your Technology

Related to email as a reactive habit is the frequency with which your corporate mail client "fetches" messages. Microsoft Exchange is by far the most common email client I see in use by my corporate clients, and although it has many advantages, it also has what I consider to be a damaging flaw: Exchange Servers check for changes to files, which includes new email messages waiting to be sent or received, every thirty seconds. This option is out of the users' control and means that as long as the Outlook software is open, users are guaranteed to have new messages constantly interrupting them. Notifications of new emails can be disabled, but my experience is that very few people avail themselves of this option, often because they feel the culture requires immediate attention to every communication.

In addition to turning off the notifications, which should be encouraged at your company (even set as the default by the IT department), you can also encourage the team to work in "Offline Mode." (In Microsoft Outlook, this can usually be found on the Send/Receive ribbon.) This means that messages that are sent will not be delivered until Offline Mode is disabled, but the productivity gains of Offline Mode far outweigh the slight delay of sending messages.

What Is "Real Work?"

There is an argument to be made that email changed the very nature of "real work," but in an unstructured, inefficient way rather than an intentional, thoughtful way. Computer science professor and author Cal Newport, writing in the *Harvard Business Review*, says:

> *It's important to remember that no blue ribbon committee or*

brilliant executive ever sat down and decided that this workflow [email] would make businesses more productive or employees more satisfied. It instead just emerged as an instinctual reaction to a disruptive new technology. Like the employees at 1980s IBM, one day we looked up and noticed that what we meant by "real work" had shifted radically under our feet.[44]

Newport proposes eliminating internal email and substituting it with the low-tech idea of using "office hours," like the kind used in academia, because synchronous communication is more efficient. I agree with the premise, and in case you're thinking, "We couldn't possibly eliminate email," he also makes a compelling argument that all the reasons you may be thinking of for why it wouldn't work are in reality reasons why you just think it would be harder. The basis for this argument is that thoughtfully planning work in a more strategic way *is* harder than an unstructured, ad hoc approach, but it's also more efficient.

A methodology for implementing a solution similar to "office hours" is the concept of "Talk To," explained in Chapter 4 of Personal Productivity Secrets.

Another, perhaps more modern, approach to managing email, especially internal email, is to take advantage of a group communication tool like Slack (www.slack.com) or HipChat (www.hipchat.com). These tools are designed to take important information out of personal inboxes and store it instead in a corporate resource that anyone can access. Private messaging is also available, but progress reports, answers to common questions, status updates, and other bits of information that are needed throughout the organization are made available in a structured, organized, and logical way, eliminating much of the back and forth that is common for email.

However, when implementing new tools, leadership must be thoughtful and deliberate in determining policies and practices, and conveying these, along with training, on the new tools. I see many companies attempt to solve problems by implementing new tools like group communication software, or project management software, sales software, or instant messaging software, but they end up just creating more problems. When considering any new technology, ask the following questions:

- ➤ What problem do we expect this tool to solve?
- ➤ How widespread is this problem?
- ➤ What other solutions, besides new technology, could solve this problem?
- ➤ Have we asked the people experiencing the problem for their recommendations for a solution?
- ➤ How will this new tool fit into the existing workflow of those who will use it?
- ➤ Are the users on board with this proposed technology solution?
- ➤ If implementing this technology is a success, what will that look like?

More on this in my Harvard Business Review article "Unless You Have Productivity Skills, Productivity Tools are Useless."

Once the determination is made to implement new technology, clear instruction is necessary as to when, and under what circumstances, that tool should be used. Otherwise the result will be yet *more* communication (e.g., sending an instant message to tell someone you sent him or her an email). In addition, typical "software training" often explains the "mechanical" how—"click here to make this happen"—but not the "logical" how. For example, I know the mechanics of using a golf club. I know to hold the grip end and swing the flat end at the ball. But when I swing, I miss the ball every time. I was taught the mechanics, but I still don't really know how to use the club.

Often, we view new tools as the cause of the problem, but if you avoid these pitfalls, new tools can absolutely be a solution.

Eliminate Inappropriate Hardware

I see my clients making another common mistake that prevents focused and undistracted time: allowing employees to have two or more computer monitors. This behavior not only condones constant distraction but also actually encourages it. An appropriate reason to have more than one monitor is for jobs that require extra "real estate" to do effectively—for example, graphic designers who need their design on one screen, and their graphic components or color palette on the second screen. However, I find that dual monitors are increasingly common for everyone in the office, and the way they are being used is to have email open and constantly downloading on one screen, and "real work" on the second screen. If the work done at your organization requires sustained focus of more than a minute or two at a time (and whose doesn't?!), then the presence of two monitors is preventing this focus most, or perhaps all, of the time.

Change Habits and Assumptions That Poison Culture

Email doesn't disrupt us only at work; it creeps into our off-hours. Consider this scenario: Around 11 p.m. one night, you realize there's a key step your team needs to take on a current project. So you dash off an email to the team members while you're thinking about it. No time like the present, right?

> **Do your company practices and expectations support efficient, balanced, and productive use of email?**

Wrong. I've seen over the past decade how after-hours emails speed up corporate cultures—and that, in turn, chips away at creativity, innovation, and true productivity. If this is a common behavior for you, you're missing the opportunity to get some distance from work—distance that's critical to the fresh perspective you need as the leader. Sometimes executives send after-hours messages because senior leaders are expected to work longer hours. Sometimes they do it because they have schedules that are more flexible. Sometimes they do it because they fall prey to the same issues as their employees. But this practice is damaging when leadership employs it because when the boss is working, the team members feel like they also should be working.

As a leader, consider your own habits. If you're working late because your hours are more flexible, leave the messages in your draft folder to be sent in the

> **Being connected in off-hours during busy times is the sign of a high performer. Never disconnecting is a sign of a workaholic. And there is a difference.**

morning, or take advantage of a "delay send" feature or app that will enable the messages to be delivered at a future time that you designate. If you're working extended hours because you think your job requires it, you might be part of the problem. Everything discussed so far about the optimal requirements for knowledge work applies especially to leaders.

Email Scheduling Solutions

Although the steps vary, most email programs and services include options for scheduling messages to be sent at a later time:

- **Microsoft Outlook**: Select Delay Delivery in the Options tab of the message.

- **Apple Mail**: Try a third-party service called MailButler (www.feingeist.io/mailbutler).

- **Gmail**: Consider the popular app Boomerang (www.boomeranggmail.com). (Note: I'm not a fan of the Boomerang feature that allows you to have a message resent to you at a later date. There's nothing more inefficient than reading the same message more than once.)

The next time the urge strikes to send that 11 p.m. email, think about the message you'd *like* to convey. Do you intend for your staff to reply to you immediately? Or are you just sending the email because you're thinking about it at the moment and want to get it done before you forget? If it's the former, you're intentionally chaining your employees to the office 24/7. If it's the latter, you're *unintentionally* chaining your employees to the office 24/7. Either way, this isn't a good situation for you, your employees, or your company culture. Being connected in off-hours during busy times is the sign of a high performer. Never disconnecting is a sign of a workaholic. And there is a difference.

Regardless of your intent, I've found through my experience with hundreds of companies that there are two reasons late-night email habits spread from the boss to her team:

> **Ambition:** If the boss is emailing late at night or on weekends, most employees think a late-night response is required—or that they'll impress you if they respond immediately. Even if just a couple of your employees share this belief, it could spread through your whole team. A casual mention in a meeting, "When we were emailing last night . . ." is all it takes. After all, everyone is looking for an edge in his or her career.

> **Attention:** There are lots of people who have no intention of "working" when they aren't at work. But they have poor attention-management skills. They're so accustomed to multitasking, and so used to constant distractions, that regardless of what else they're doing, they find their fingers mindlessly tapping the smartphone icons that connect them to their emails, texts, and social media. If an employee is in the habit of constantly checking email and other communication channels all day, that habit is hard to pause at the end of the workday. Your late-night communication feeds that bad habit.

It has also become socially acceptable to email, text, or IM our colleagues about work during off-hours even though we would rarely call about work matters during those times. Presumably, these new communication tools seem less intrusive than a ringing phone, but the disruptions are still damaging. So the employee's constant checking habits, plus her assumptions of expectations, combine with the leader's circumstances, and voilà:

It only takes one employee engaging in harmful email behaviors to create pressure among other employees to adopt these behaviors.

The result is a perfect—and often unintentional—storm that leaves a damaged work culture in its wake.

This tendency to stay connected—whether being tethered to email at work or sending and responding to email after hours—is often viewed as required by the employer, or as necessary to keep up with the demands of the job when, in fact, it's simply a reflection of the habits, behaviors, and assumptions of the employee. Researchers now call it *telepressure*, and define it as, "an urge to quickly respond to emails, texts and voice-mails—regardless of whatever else is happening or whether one is even 'at work.'"[45]

It only takes one employee engaging in harmful email behaviors to create pressure among other employees to adopt these behaviors, and soon the pace at the company is heightened, frantic, constant, and conducive to burnout. Some employers are guilty of inciting this. In many cases, however, leadership does not mandate the behavior, it's just presumed to be expected, not only by the employees but also often in news articles and even in research studies. If the leadership is guilty of anything, it's of allowing the culture to evolve organically based on bad habits.

Prioritize Time to Recharge

Being always "on" hurts results. If after-hours emailing is the norm in your company, you're doing damage to your employees and, not incidentally, to yourself. When employees are constantly monitoring their email after work hours—whether due to a fear of missing something from you or because they are addicted to their devices—they are missing out on essential downtime that brains need. When work is always with us and our brains never have time to recharge, we deplete our creativity, motivation, and ability to make connections and insights. This leaves us no time for reflection and the thoughtful application of knowledge and experience. All of these are the very factors that are the basis of hiring decisions and are necessary for high-quality knowledge work.

Always-on cultures actually sabotage productivity. The research has shown that more downtime correlates to more benefits.[46] Overworked, stressed-out, fearful employees are not a good source of creative ideas. In a summary of studies for Innovation Management, a Swedish consultancy company, Gaia Grant, author of *Who Killed Creativity . . . and How Can We Get It Back?* (Wrightbooks, 2012), writes, "Creative thinking requires a relaxed state, the ability to think through options at a slow pace and the openness to explore different alternatives without fear."[47] According to Jen Spencer, founder of The Creative Executive (www.creative-executive.com), "play" is an important component in creativity, and if all people do is work, then they're crowding out "play times" that are important to generating innovative ideas. She tells me, "When we balance work with play, it's like cross-training our minds and our soul. Play is about enjoyment, relaxation, and recreation, which gives our minds the ability to replenish the resources we need to be strategic, make new connections, and innovate." Put another way, telepressure and innovation cannot coexist.

Institutional Changes: Be Intentional About Email

Company leaders can keep unhealthy assumptions about email and other communication from taking root. They should thoughtfully identify desired behaviors, clearly communicate those expectations, and provide training to address them. This creates a culture based on intention. The following steps will put you on the right path:

1. *Get clear with your leadership team about the company values and beliefs related to communication and downtime, and on which communication practices support or detract from these beliefs and values.* For example, if you say that your company values employees' well-being, how does that jibe with a company culture that encourages around-the-clock availability via email? The (often unconscious) belief that more work equals more success is difficult to overcome, but the truth is that this belief is neither beneficial nor sustainable. Long work hours actually decrease both productivity and engagement.[48] I've seen that leaders often believe theoretically in downtime, but they also want to keep company objectives moving forward—which seems like it requires constant communication.

2. *Decide what your company's expectations and best practices will be concerning email and other communication tools.* For example, is after-hours communication appropriate? If so, in what manner (Email? Text? Phone?) and under what circumstances? If this discussion leads to the conclusion that constant availability is required to meet the goals of the organization, that's a corporate issue that needs to be addressed. This may be an acceptable short-term situation, but it's not sustainable long term.[49]

> If you say that your company values employees' well-being, how does that jibe with a company culture that encourages around-the-clock availability via email?

I advocate the following two key practices:

- Don't use email for urgent or time-sensitive communication.
- Be clear that periodically closing email and setting instant messengers to "away" is encouraged, and an immediate response to emails is not necessary.

3. *Clearly communicate your email expectations and best practices, and establish them as policy.*

4. *As leaders, model the desired email behaviors yourselves.* If you still immediately respond to all emails even though your new policy makes clear this isn't required of employees, you're sending mixed messages.

5. *Have your IT department apply settings to turn off all notifications of new email.*

6. *Review how people are using a second computer monitor, and examine whether it is supporting or sabotaging their productivity and attention.*

Vynamic: Creating an Email Culture That Works

Vynamic, a successful healthcare consultancy in Philadelphia led by Dan Calista, offers an example of an email policy that promotes a healthy work culture. They created a policy they call "zmail," which discourages email between 10 p.m. and 7 a.m. during the week and all day on weekends.

The policy doesn't discourage work during these times, nor does it prohibit communication. If an after-hours message seems necessary, the staff is forced to assess whether it's important enough to require a phone call.

If employees choose to work during off-hours, zmail encourages them to avoid putting their habits onto others by sending emails during this time; they simply save the messages as drafts to be manually sent later, or they program their email clients to automatically send the messages during work hours. This policy creates alignment between the stated belief that downtime is important and the habits of the staff that contribute to the culture.

Leaders like Dan Calista have found a way to balance a growing business with a healthy life for himself and his team. So question your assumptions about being always available. It's human nature to operate based on assumptions—sometimes assumptions we don't even realize we're holding. For example, if everyone at your organization seems to be keeping long hours, you might find yourself doing the same, based on the vague belief that if everyone is doing it, you must "have to." However, there is certainly no hard evidence to support the idea that those who are the most available or work the longest hours are the most successful. In fact, some executives have realized that it's really only the illusion of constant availability that's important.

In a study of more than one hundred employees at a global consulting firm, three types of workers emerged: those who embraced the demanding culture and worked long hours (who were seen as high performers), those who pushed back and insisted on lighter workloads and more flexible hours (resulting in negative performance reviews), and those who gave the impression of working the long hours but actually achieved the benefits of a lighter schedule without asking for it. This third group received the same praise and rate of promotion as those in the first group.[50] The illusion itself is detrimental, but these executives prove that while the assumption may be that around-the-clock work is necessary, the reality is something different.

Conclusion

Like most technology, the problems related to email typically stem from the way it's used rather than with the technology itself. But setting your company up for success requires thought and intention with regard to the way email is used in your organization. Leaving it up to your employees to "figure it out for themselves" leaves your corporate culture, and the results your organization produces, to chance.

The pace of business has increased in the twenty-first century. But if conventional wisdom now says that constant work is necessary for professional success, I can't think of a more important time to buck convention.

Action Items

These are specific steps that will help you put the information in this chapter to use immediately. Most can be implemented relatively quickly and easily and can pay big returns:

1. Look at whether your company's communications practices support your beliefs and values about employee downtime and well-being. Specifically, how much email and communication happens at night, on weekends, and during employee vacations? Break the habit of sending after-hours emails by using your drafts folder or a "delay send" feature or app.

2. Stop using email for urgent or time-sensitive information. Insist on the same from other leadership. When you see others doing this, use it as a teachable moment and point out an alternative means of communication.

3. Be clear that people should not expect immediate responses to emails.

4. To get less email, make full use of your email client's rules, filters, and junk mail functionality. Assess the use of "replies to all," and system generated messages.

5. Consider rolling out SpamDrain, Throttle, and Unroll.me to help employees filter and bundle messages and unsubscribe from mailing lists.

6. Evaluate the use of email "cc" as a means to "keep people in the loop." This is likely not the most effective behavior.

7. Recognize email as "work" and communicate this throughout the organization. Regularly make room in your own schedule for processing email, and support your team members as they do the same.

8. Encourage working offline when doing work, including the work in email.

9. Have your IT department shut off all email notifications on computers and smartphones.

10. Consider whether a version of Cal Newport's "office hours" idea might help reduce the volume of email in your office.

11. Have your IT manager review group communication tools like Slack and HipChat. If they recommend implementation, insist on a proposal for not only rollout, but also technical training *and* behavioral training (i.e., when will this communication channel be chosen over other tools).

12. Limit the use of multiple monitors. They increase the temptation to leave email open at all times. Only employees who truly need the extra screen, such as graphic designers, should have more than one monitor.

Takeaways You Can Tweet

Here are important points of the chapter summarized so that they are easy to digest, but also so that you can conveniently share the information with your followers on Twitter or on other social media outlets. Follow and participate in the conversation online using *#workwithout-walls*, and/or my handle, @mnthomas.

- ❏ Bad email habits result in stressed and frantic corporate cultures.
- ❏ You can't 'squeeze in' email and be effective. It's real work that takes real time.
- ❏ Start leaving more room in your schedule to handle email.
- ❏ To get email under control, don't forget rules, filters, and junk mail features of your email client.
- ❏ If you need email help, try blocking, bundling, and unsubscribing services.
- ❏ Skim email from handheld devices only. Your computer is too distracting.
- ❏ When you process email, turn off the download of new messages.
- ❏ Break the after-hours email habit: It hurts team productivity.
- ❏ Turn off email notifications and work offline sometimes. And encourage your team to do this too.
- ❏ Slack, Hipchat, Throttle, and SpamDrain could help ease your team's email burden.
- ❏ More than one computer monitor drains productivity.
- ❏ Leaders' email habits set the tone for the team.
- ❏ Bad email habits spread through teams. The solution is to get clear on expectations and best practices.
- ❏ Being connected 24/7 is a sign that you have 'telepressure.' And it's hurting your work.
- ❏ If you're 'always on,' you'll be less creative.
- ❏ You can't value employees AND keep them tied to email.

Chapter 4

IS YOUR VACATION POLICY BROKEN?

Time off pays off . . . I firmly believe that time
spphanded spent away to refresh and refocus is really
not time off. It's just time better spent.[51]

—JOHN DONAHOE, FORMER EBAY CEO

TODAY'S environment of work without walls gives us more freedom to do our jobs where and when we want. But it also means that the walls that protected the rest of our lives from work intrusions are falling. One place that this phenomenon manifests is in attitudes, practices, and policies regarding vacation time.

Although doing more with less—and doing it 24/7/365—has seemed like the corporate mantra of the past two decades, there is a growing body of evidence about the benefits of vacation to our physical, mental, and fiscal health.

Valuing Vacation

An overlooked fact about vacation is the return on investment. If you offer your employees paid vacation, then you are essentially paying for their opportunity to recharge, refresh, and refocus. If they are available for work issues when on vacation, then they aren't really getting those benefits for which you're paying. With new perspective comes new insight, and they can't get a fresh perspective on something they never really step away from for more than eight to ten hours at a time (while sleeping).

Studies show that time away from work is good for weight and cardiovascular health; it lowers cortisol levels and blood pressure; and it may aid in recovery from diseases such as cancer.[52]

New research from Shawn Achor, author of *The Happiness Advantage* (Crown Business, 2010), and Project: Time Off (www.projecttimeoff.com) also shows that contrary to conventional wisdom, vacation just might be great for our careers, including increasing our odds of being promoted and being perceived as more productive.[53] And most people accept this—at least intellectually. A 2013 study conducted by the Society for Human Resource Management (SHRM) for the U.S. Travel Association shows that huge majorities of American workers say paid time off:[54]

➤ Helps them relax and recharge (90 percent)

➤ Offers the opportunity to do what they enjoy (88 percent)

➤ Makes them happier (85 percent)

➤ Improves their concentration and productivity (66 percent)

➤ Results in greater satisfaction at work (61 percent)

Additionally, 91 percent of senior leaders agree that employees who use their paid time off return recharged and renewed, ready to work more efficiently and productively.[55]

Coinciding with the increasing evidence of the personal and professional benefits of vacation is recent discussion in the business media that because "work" no longer adheres to the traditional 9-to-5 schedule, and because technology allows us to be connected anywhere and everywhere, perhaps those longer work hours should be reconciled with more time off.

Examining the Latest Idea in Vacation Policy

The cumulative effect of this evidence and discussion is a small number of companies substituting policies that prescribe vacation time with an "unlimited vacation-time" policy, in an effort to enable employees to make work-life balance decisions that supposedly "work for them." Recognizable names such as Virgin, Netflix, Evernote, Expedia, and Motley Fool are leading the charge. The task of vacation tracking is eliminated from to-do lists all over the office, and there is some evidence that a more open time-off policy can help make a company attractive when recruiting new hires. Netflix, at least, seems to think the policy is a boon to the business, reporting that people can spend more time innovating rather than accounting for their time.[56]

The downside of this approach, however, is a lot of pressure on employees to ensure, as Richard Branson of Virgin puts it, that "they are only going to do it when they feel a hundred percent comfortable that they and their team are up to date on every project and that their absence will not in any way damage the business—or, for that matter, their careers!"[57] This seems like a high bar when everyone always has too much to do. In fact, this philosophy could create so much pressure that employees actually feel less comfortable taking vacation. Early studies show that unlimited vacation-time policies don't actually increase the number of vacation days taken and can give employees the impression that the company is taking advantage of them.[58] *The Chicago Tribune* announced a change to a more flexible vacation policy and then quickly rescinded it, saying that it created confusion and concern within the company.[59]

Although an unlimited vacation-day policy may be a useful component of the twenty-first-century office, it misses the point. For one thing, American workers already forfeit a large percentage of their existing paid time off.

> *Unlimited vacation-time policy misses the point.*

Project: Time Off estimates workers forfeited 169 million days off in 2013.[60] That means that the specific amount of time employees are "allowed" really isn't the issue. Also, I hear my clients say that they work long hours before vacation in preparation for being away and long hours when they get back in order to catch up. So really, the "vacation time" is more like "flex time," with many of the hours just being shifted. Lastly, when workers "use" their vacation time, they don't *really* disconnect from the office. In my work as a productivity trainer, I see a common expectation within companies that vacationing staffers will still be available—another example of the "telepressure" I referred to in chapter 3. So it makes sense that a 2014 report from career-community company Glassdoor says that 61 percent of employees work while on vacation.[61]

Acknowledge the "Work Martyr" Syndrome

The U.S. Travel Association identified that workers have several reasons for not taking time off and for working on vacation. These qualities are symptoms of what they call the "work martyr." The study uncovered the following:

> ➤ Forty percent of employees are afraid of the mountain of work they'll face when they return to work after time off.

> ➤ Thirty-five percent say they are the only ones who can do their jobs.

> ➤ Twenty-five percent fear losing their jobs or being seen as replaceable if they take time off.[62]

There is evidence that these feelings of the work martyr may be justified. The U.S. Travel Association report goes on to say the following:

> ➤ Sixty-six percent of employees say they hear no communication, negative messages, or mixed messages about taking paid time off.

> ➤ Twenty-eight percent of senior leaders find it difficult to approve paid time-off requests.

> ➤ Thirty-two percent of leaders worry that vacation time puts an extra burden on other employees.[63]

What I often hear from my clients is something like, *"Why take a vacation at all? What's the point when I have to check email from the beach just to keep up with the constant stream of work and avoid a massive backlog when I return?"* In other words, workers feel the need to be "always on" to keep up with workplace demands. It's no wonder, when even ostensible "encouragements" to take vacation, such as this excerpt from an article from *Harvard Business Review* about being a "pro-vacation manager," contain advice like this:

> "Put away your devices while you're on vacation. Designate a couple of consistent times per day, so your team knows when you will be checking in."[64]

So in short, this "encouragement" advises you to put away your devices while you're on vacation—until you take them out again multiple times a day so that you can work—and apparently vacation activities will need to be arranged around these regularly scheduled work check-ins!

Always-on behavior is detrimental to creativity and innovation because crucial characteristics, such as willpower, motivation, and inspiration, become limited when you don't take time away from your job. A vacation allows you distance from your work and your everyday life that provides a new perspective, a creativity boost, and a clarity of thought that gets buried by the fast pace of your daily routine.

> *A workplace culture that discourages time off isn't sustainable. And, in the long run, it isn't more productive.*

The success of company leaders, and all knowledge workers, depends on the wisdom, experience, and unique perspective that you bring to your work. Your supply of motivation and unique creativity is not endless, and you can't get distance from work if you set aside time during your vacation to check in with your office, either by email or phone. You may think you're taking only a short time out of your vacation, but the truth is that reconnecting to work periodically during your time off means that your mind stays engaged in the office, effectively thwarting your opportunity to gain distance, fresh perspective, and recharge of motivation and creativity. John Donahoe, former CEO of eBay, summed it up best when he said, "Time off pays off . . . I firmly believe that time spent away to refresh and refocus is really not time off. It's just time better spent."[65]

Align Belief with Behavior

Furthermore, a report by small business loan–provider OnDeck finds that most business owners don't take vacation in the first *ten years* of business, and, when they do take vacation, only 15 percent disconnect entirely.[66] The culture of vacation is set at the top, and it appears that small business owners, accounting for tens of millions of employees, are setting a standard of "no vacation." The same point from chapter 3 applies: although senior leaders may understand *intellectually* that paid time off improves performance, this understanding can be overshadowed by a stronger (and often subconscious) belief that more work equals more success. But a workplace culture that discourages time off, explicitly or implicitly, isn't sustainable. And, in the long run, it isn't more productive.

Time away from the office to stroll on a beach or wander through a museum isn't just something that's nice for your employees to have. Neuroscientists have found that it's something our brains need to be productive. It's the "restorative mode" mentioned in chapter 2 that promotes the kind of mental state conducive to new ideas and fresh insights. This mental state leads to creativity and innovation, and missing out means that employees run low on the very qualities they need for success as a knowledge worker, including willpower, motivation, and inspiration.

Bob Chapman is CEO of $2-plus billion Barry-Wehmiller and author of *Everybody Matters: The Extraordinary Power of Caring for Your People Like Family* (Portfolio, 2015). His website sums up his approach of "Truly Human Leadership":

> *Bob Chapman imagines a world where every person matters. Imagine a world full of caring work environments in which people can realize their gifts, apply and develop their talents,*

and feel a genuine sense of fulfillment for their contributions. Chapman imagines a world in which people leave work each day fulfilled and are better spouses, fathers, mothers, sons, daughters, neighbors, citizens of the world. Because everyone—including you—matters.[67]

There are many other successful entrepreneurs and executives, many of whom are referenced throughout this book, who prove that a balance of success and downtime is still possible. Additional examples include Jared Brown, the cofounder of software company Hubstaff, who writes in *Forbes* about prioritizing his family, making time for exercise, and taking the weekends off.[68] Arianna Huffington wrote a *New York Times* best seller called *Thrive* (Harmony, 2014), and she refers to "thriving"—which includes mindfulness and taking care of your well-being—as a critical metric of success. It took her collapsing of exhaustion to come to this realization, but rather than make the same mistake, we can learn from her experience. True vacation time, without any work, is an important ingredient in all of these examples.

Institutional Changes: Create a Comprehensive Vacation Plan

Be mindful that, as a leader, your behavior influences the culture of the organization. If you (or your people) work incessantly and meet your professional goals, but you've done so at the expense of your personal life, your family, or your mental or physical health—is that the kind of "success" you aspire to? And is that what you want for your employees? Even if you believe that your employees' single-minded focus on work will help you achieve your company goals, in the first place I hope this book is beginning to convince you that you're wrong. Second, you'll eventually pay the price in employee burnout, turnover, and difficulty in recruiting the best people.

For companies to reap the benefits of their investment in vacation time for their employees, the solution has to be more comprehensive than simply adjusting the old-fashioned policy. It's not sufficient to just state that employees need to take time away from work to restore. Company leaders must do more than talk.

Show Support for Time Off

If you think you have a neutral stance on vacation time by neither vocally encouraging it nor discouraging it, employees may interpret your silence on the topic as meaning you implicitly discourage time off. Likewise, if you reach out by phone or email to an employee who's on vacation, you're communicating an expectation that she should work during her time off—even if you argue that she "should know" that you don't expect a reply until she's back at work.

Here are other ways that leaders can show support for time off, help employees feel good about taking time to recharge, and reap the benefits of increased productivity and fresh creativity inside the organization:

> *If you contact an employee who's on vacation, you're communicating an expectation that she should work during her time off—even if you argue that she "should know" that you don't expect a reply until she's back at work.*

➤ **Engage in a frank discussion with your leadership team about what managers and executives truly believe about time off** and whether they discourage, even inadvertently, using vacation days or fully unplugging while on vacation. Investigate whether your workplace culture, leadership behaviors, and employee assumptions are in line with those beliefs.

➤ **Use your own paid time off, and don't check email while you're on vacation.** You'll get all the restorative benefits of vacation yourself, of course, and you'll be modeling healthy behavior for employees. Encourage everyone, especially the leaders and influencers at your organization, to do the same.

➤ **Be clear in communicating support for taking paid time off and being fully away from work during vacations** because, in today's work environment, failing to encourage vacation time (or failing to unplug) is awfully close to actually discouraging vacation time.

➤ **Help employees acquire the workflow-management skills and tools addressed in chapter 2.** This will facilitate their ability to set their own boundaries, better understand their priorities and deadlines, and impose their own limits about vacation time. These aren't skills taught in school, and as technology and communication channels proliferate, it's getting harder and harder.

➤ **Implement a policy that a manager going on vacation can choose a trusted staffer to take on his responsibilities.** This provides incentive to the manager not to check in because that would be perceived as a lack of confidence in the staffer. Additionally, the staff person has an opportunity to grow. (One of my clients told me that this "Boss for a Day/Week" was a common practice at IBM in the 1980s.)

Harness Technology in Support of Vacation

In addition to showing support and modeling the benefits of disconnecting, technology solutions and innovative polices are another option. For example, it's easy to hide or disable email on some smartphones, which can help workers resist the temptation to check in.

Smartphone Instructions

Android users can disable the email sync while they're on vacation, so no new messages arrive. This can be found in "Settings→Accounts→Sync, and then deselect "Auto-Sync." Iphone users can find detailed instructions at http://regainyourtime.com/how-to-make-the-most-of-your-labor-day-holiday-weekend-or-any-vacation/

Enlist your IT staff to help make sure your employees actually renew and recharge during their downtime instead of being tied to their email. For example, all staff should be shown how to schedule outgoing mail (as described in the previous chapter) so that people can write messages whenever they like, but those messages only get sent during business hours or when a colleague has returned from his or her vacation. Additionally, all staff should know how to put an out-of-office message on their email and their voicemail. (I recommend the message start one day before departure and end at least one day after return to provide a buffer that makes it easier to transition.) The IT staff could also change a vacationing staffer's email and voicemail passwords so that he can't retrieve messages while on vacation, even if he wants to. However, these solutions don't address the anxiety a staffer might have at the prospect of returning to a mountain of work, so you should consider other techniques to alleviate that concern.

Reduce "Out of Office Anxiety"

One way is to model Daimler's policy, recently adopted by Huffington Post as well, and offer employees an opportunity to have their messages deleted while they are away, using an auto-responder similar to this one:

> "Thank you for your message. I am on vacation, so please direct your communication to XX in my absence, or resend it after X date when I will be back in the office. Your initial message has been deleted in my absence."

When I share this policy with my CEO audiences, there is usually at least one person in the room who grumbles, "That's the fastest way to send my customers to my competition." In fact, however, the exact opposite appears to be true. Consider this report from the BBC:

> Apparently, people receiving such a notification rarely get angry. "The response is basically 99% positive, because everybody says, 'That's a real nice thing, I would love to have that too,'" Daimler spokesman Oliver Wihofszki told BBC Radio 4's Today programme. Holiday envy has been replaced by corporate email policy envy. The response on Twitter has also been overwhelmingly positive.[69]

Another policy worthy of consideration is the one employed by Full Contact, a Colorado technology company, that it calls "Paid Paid Vacation." In addition to paid time off, every employee gets $7,500 per year that must be used for vacation: Disconnecting is required, and working while on this vacation is prohibited. Besides recognizing the benefits available upon return from vacation, Full Contact CEO and cofounder Bart Lorang identified some unexpected benefits that occur before the time is even used! The following is from the Full Contact blog:

If people know they will be disconnecting and going off the grid for an extended period of time, they might actually keep that in mind as they help build the company. For example:

> ➤ *They might empower direct reports to make more decisions.*
> ➤ *They might be less likely to create a special script that . . . only lives on their machine.*
> ➤ *They might document their code a bit better.*
> ➤ *They might contribute to the Company Wiki and share knowledge.*

Get the picture? At the end of the day, the company will improve.[70]

Examine Existing Vacation Policies

In addition to implementing some of the preceding suggestions, you might still choose to eliminate your formal vacation policy that requires specifying and tracking the number of days off. It's important to ensure however, that "no vacation policy" doesn't actually mean "no vacation!" For advice about things to consider before implementing an unlimited vacation-day policy, I turned to human resources executive Melissa Bixby, principal in HumInt (www.humintllc.com), an HR consulting firm:

> ➤ *Eliminating a formal vacation policy works best for professional-level (exempt) employees,* who are typically more independent and self-managing. They are used to receiving limited feedback, setting goals, and hitting deadlines, so regulating their own time off wouldn't require a major shift in behavior.
> ➤ *This type of program is not well suited to a workforce comprised of predominantly non-exempt employees,* who are typically highly supervised and take direction on most daily tasks. In addition, the Fair Labor Standards Act

requires hours of non-exempt employees be tracked and documented.

➤ *As with any flextime arrangement, the company needs to have a strong philosophy about goal setting and managing accountability.* Leadership needs to be able to measure results based on the needs of the business and its strategic goals so that an employee's success is not evaluated based on hours spent in the office.

Advice on measuring results is covered in Chapters 2, 6, and 7.

➤ *Most human resource policies are written in consideration of the small percentage of employees who might be prone to abuse,* and this situation won't be the exception. There will be employees who will take advantage of the "unlimited" nature offered when there is no specific limit to vacation days, so leadership should consider how to address potential abuse before issuing the policy. The strong culture of accountability mentioned earlier can help in this regard. Including a suggested maximum number of vacation days, instead of offering a truly "unlimited" number, can also be beneficial, especially in the beginning.

The new world of work without walls requires new attention to the policies and practices at your company about vacation. Examining the issues in this chapter, and implementing the suggestions, will enable you to be intentional about this aspect of your corporate culture.

- -

Conclusion

Employee downtime and vacation is an important component of company culture, and the new realities of work without walls require careful and thorough consideration and implementation to ensure that culture is not left to chance. Productivity ultimately suffers when employees skimp on time off or work while they're on vacation. Give your staff the support, policies, and tools they need to truly get away and recharge.

To be more productive and efficient is to make the best use of the resources available to you. In your quest toward productivity, for yourself or your company, don't neglect the most important resources, which are neither time nor money, but body and mind. When your work precludes physical and emotional well-being, your pursuit of productivity will be destined to fail.

📋 Action Items

These are specific steps that will help you put the information in this chapter to use immediately. Most can be implemented relatively quickly and easily and can pay big returns:

1. Discuss employee vacations with other leadership, including ways to encourage employees to take vacation. Decide that employees should not be expected to check in when they are on vacation. Weigh various policies that ensure both, and implement the right solutions for your organization.

2. Don't call, email, or otherwise reach out to employees who are on vacation—even if you don't expect a reply until they are back. Insist other employees follow this same practice.

3. Use your own vacation days and unplug fully while you're off. If you don't, it's hard for employees to feel comfortable taking time off and unplugging from work themselves.

4. Ensure that training helps employees acquire the work-flow-management skills and tools required to set their own boundaries and impose their own limits about vacation time.

5. Allow managers going on vacation to delegate their responsibilities to trusted staffers. Empower them with complete authority while the manager is gone.

6. Explore technology solutions that keep employees from checking email while they're away, such as changing their password, disabling messages on their smartphones, or automatically deleting messages received.

7. Evaluate whether policies like unlimited vacation or Full Contact's "Paid Paid Vacation" are a good fit for your company.

💬 Takeaways You Can Tweet

Here are important points of the chapter summarized so that they are easy to digest, but also so that you can conveniently share the information with your followers on Twitter or on other social media outlets. Follow and participate in the conversation online using *#workwithout-walls*, and/or my handle, @mnthomas.

- ❑ Studies show vacation is good for health, may increase chance of promotion, and cause us to be seen as more productive.
- ❑ 40% of employees are afraid of the mountain of work they'll face when they return to work from time off.
- ❑ Unlimited vacation-time policies can be good for recruitment but can also create pressure and confusion.
- ❑ If you think you can't take vacation, you might be a "work martyr."
- ❑ A workplace culture that discourages time off isn't sustainable. And, in the long run, it isn't more productive.
- ❑ Ensure the behavior of your leadership matches your stated beliefs about the importance of vacation.
- ❑ It's easy to hide your email on your iPhone when you're on vacation: http://www.regainyourtime.com/how-to-make-the-most-of-your-labor-day-holiday-weekend-or-any-vacation/
- ❑ Vacation can improve the company before it's even used: anticipating it can cause knowledge sharing & empower direct reports.

Chapter 5

THE OFFICE ENVIRONMENT

*Collaboration is the essence of life. The
wind, bees and flowers work together, to
spread the pollen. Mindfulness gives us
the opportunity [for] collaboration.*[71]

—DR. AMIT RAY

OVERWHELMING evidence demon-
strates that the design of an office impacts the health,
well-being, and productivity of its occupants, and yet
those factors are rarely considered when office design and
redesign plans are being made.[72] In office buildings, the
concept of work without walls means fewer physical walls
and more open spaces, and the general consensus seems to
be that about 70 percent of workplaces use an open-office
floor plan.

Yet the quote above illustrates the paradox of open
offices: the argument in favor is that taking down the walls
and creating open spaces where employees work together
will facilitate opportunities for creative alliances that would
be difficult or impossible to fabricate. However, they also
prevent the occasion for quiet, undistracted reflection—a
component of mindfulness—in which knowledge workers
thrive.

Do Open Offices Help or Hurt Productivity?

There is research in support of the open office, showing that "it can foster collaboration, promote learning, and nurture a strong culture."[73] Employees in open-office environments often report:

➤ An increased sense of camaraderie

➤ An opportunity to make diverse connections throughout the organization

➤ An appreciation of the time to socialize with co-workers.

The researchers who have come to these conclusions—in this case, all employees of office furniture manufacturer Steelcase, writing in the October 2014 *Harvard Business Review*—claim that where there are problems, it isn't because of the open office itself; rather, its execution is to blame.

Collision Spaces

So called "collision spaces" are all the rage. This can refer to open areas for discussion that take the place of enclosed conference rooms, areas for informal gatherings such as around coffee service, or open spaces for general work. However, this idea is taken to an extreme when removing all walls inside the workspace.

Employers want to open the workplace to promote interaction and collaboration. In the quest to have people mingle productively, some companies—including Google, Samsung, and Facebook—are betting on environments that foster unstructured and unexpected partnerships. At Samsung, leaders designed the company's new US headquarters with vast open spaces. The company's hope is that giving workers from varying disciplines unstructured opportunities to mingle and interact will spark innovation.

Even as the benefits of open spaces are touted by some, though, there's a rising chorus of displeasure at open offices, both in research and anecdotally, with claims that open offices increase stress and distractions and lower productivity.

So where does that leave you if you're creating a new office space, remodeling an old one, or simply looking for ways to make the best of your current open-office layout? We'll look at the pros and cons of the open office and how you can create an environment that helps your employees thrive.

Collaboration at What Cost?

It's my belief that unless open offices are implemented with diligence and careful consideration, the drawbacks of these spaces outweigh the benefits. What we are learning both through research and mounting anecdotal evidence is that the open office fails employees in some important ways.

Research shows that employees in open offices experience impaired cognitive function due to the noise and constant interruptions.[74] And a review of more than one hundred studies revealed employees' dissatisfaction with the lack of privacy and loss of control over their surroundings

> *There is an increasing amount of evidence that the open office fails employees in some important ways.*

and interactions, plus reduced attention spans, productivity, creative thinking, concentration, and motivation.[75] Perhaps more importantly—given that collaboration is often cited as an overriding benefit of open-office plans—the studies also show that damage to productivity from office noise is *not* offset by the benefits of collaboration.[76]

The anecdotal evidence matches what research has found. Here are a few examples:

- ➤ "After nine years as a senior writer, I was forced to trade in my private office for a seat at a long, shared table. It felt like my boss had ripped off my clothes and left me standing in my skivvies."[77] Lindsey Kaufman, writing in *The Washington Post*.
- ➤ "The open-office movement is like some gigantic experiment in willful delusion."[78] Jason Feifer, writing in *Fast Company*.
- ➤ "The victims of open offices are pushing back,"[79] was the title of an article in BBC news.

➤ A particularly insightful comment on a blog states, "[Open floor plans are a] cover for the fact that most startups are A) changing too rapidly to develop appropriate communication flow, B) have no idea what appropriate communication flow would look like, and C) don't care if developers have 'information overload.'"[80]

> "The open-office movement is like some gigantic experiment in willful delusion." —Jason Feifer

➤ "That most people hate open offices is surprising at all speaks to the current trendiness of open layouts."[81] Ariel Schwartz, writing on the *Fast Company* website, FastCoExist.

What's behind all this dissatisfaction? The open office deprives workers of privacy, control, and spaces conducive to quiet, focused work.

More Openness, Less Control

Employees in an open office can feel helpless because they lack control over their environment. That helplessness can hurt satisfaction, engagement, and productivity. The open office takes away control over the following things:

➤ Space

➤ Privacy

➤ Well-being

➤ Stimulation

Control over Space

Workers crave their own space, or at least access to a place where they can feel in control of both their personal and professional information.

If workers lack their own space entirely, they're constantly distracted by having to think about their workspace every day, according to Dr. Art Markman, a social psychology professor at the University of Texas at Austin. Because it's harder for these workers to put anything on "autopilot," Markman says, they're less efficient. For example, instead of just mindlessly reaching for a pen, a worker has to disrupt his task to look for the pen cup.

Control over Privacy

Offices with no walls or only glass walls can make employees feel like they are working in a fishbowl—that they are always under scrutiny. As a result, they may spend time managing impressions: worrying about what it *looks* like they're doing instead of just focusing on their work.

> **Offices with no walls or only glass walls can make employees feel like they are working in a fishbowl.**

And it's human nature to be far less irreverent when you feel you are being watched. How does that relate to the workplace and productivity? Irreverence fosters creativity,[82] meaning the open office might be as likely to stifle creativity as foster it.

Control over Well-Being

Employees in open offices even have less control over things as basic as their wellness. Sick time has been shown to increase in open-office environments.[83] In addition to germs, stress and anxiety can be spread in open-office environments. Multiple studies have shown that if you observe anxious and highly expressive behavior, those emotions are likely to spread to you and negatively impact your performance.[84]

Control over Stimulation

All employees have the desire, or need, to control the amount of stimulation they are subjected to in the workplace. An open office takes away that control. It subjects workers to constant and competing stimuli, in the form of noise. In addition to hampering productivity, office noise can decrease motivation and increase stress chemicals in the bloodstream.[85]

Why Overheard Phone Conversations Are So Annoying

Here's a fascinating observation relayed to me by Dr. Art Markman about a common distraction in an open office: hearing your coworkers' phone conversations:

> Studies show that overhearing only half of a conversation is much more distracting than hearing the entire conversation. This is because it's much easier for our brains to ignore predictable things, like the back-and-forth of a conversation. However, hearing only one side of the conversation means that there is no predictable pattern, resulting in noise that is much harder to ignore.

All the stimuli and interruptions of an open office overload the senses and increase cortisol and adrenaline.[86] Because they're distracted, workers constantly switch between tasks, which requires them to do more work to achieve a quality result. And the sense that they're never alone and free from distractions can make workers anxious and—you guessed it—less productive.

Focused Work Requires Quiet Spaces

Our tolerance for stimulation, and our need to control it, varies with the type of work we are doing. My study of attention has led me to think of it in terms of three types:

➤ **Stimulus-driven attention**: When doing less-intense work, such as filling out expense reports or cleaning out our inboxes, we tend to welcome interruptions from the routine nature of the task, and therefore we allow our attention to be stimulus driven.

   Jobs that require more reaction, such as support positions, require more time spent in stimulus-driven attention. Collaborative tasks can also benefit from stimulus-driven attention, and workers often prefer to do these tasks in an open setting, which is a more likely environment for stimulus-driven attention.

➤ **Focused attention**: Writing, deep thought, and detail work are examples that require focused attention—when our need for control over our environment is at its height. We seek to avoid interruption and stimulation, so quiet, private spaces are best. Most knowledge work jobs require at least some amount of focused attention.

➤ **Restorative attention:** Every brain needs a time-out, where our brains can be allowed to wander, and I think of this as "restorative attention." This is the time when we are protected from excessive stimulation, and we're also not actively focusing on anything in particular. It's during these times when we can let our minds wander. Often these are the times when insights are generated; when you are not actively thinking about something, but your brain has a chance to process, reflect, and consolidate.[87]

The products of knowledge work are creativity, communication, and decisions, none of which thrive in noisy, shared workspaces where interruptions abound. Your knowledge workers need time in focused attention and restorative attention to deliver the creativity and insights for which you pay them. But private, quiet spaces that support those kinds of attention are missing in most open-office settings.

As a leader, you'll drive better results when you're deliberate about giving employees an environment that supports their need for control and offers different spaces to do different kinds of work. Not only does the environment need to support these issues, but the culture needs to as well. Employees need to believe in the benefit of the quiet spaces, and this is difficult to achieve if the leadership doesn't model the behavior or dedicate the appropriate space.

Institutional Changes: Designing or Redesigning an Office

There are many ways to plan for a supportive environment and influence the culture in a way that is favorable to employee productivity.

Considering a Move to an Open-Office Floor Plan

When deciding to restructure to an open office, many companies consider efficiency in terms of cost per square foot, an objective metric that works well in financial reporting. Indeed, the only uncontested information about open-office floor plans is that they reduce the square footage requirement for companies. But, when factoring productivity into the equation, this economic consideration is too simple because it ignores how the design of a space affects performance.

If you are creating a new office or redesigning an existing one, my advice is to buck the trend for open floor plans. Collaboration and innovation are important, but as this chapter illustrates, there is no clear evidence to support that open-office floor plans increase these characteristics within an organization, and there's ample evidence pointing to detrimental effects. Here is an interesting piece of information to consider with regard to innovation: Group discussions can actually dampen creativity and originality. "Group-think" takes over via a process called "anchoring," which means that early ideas have disproportionate influence over the rest of the conversation.[88] Idea-generation is best done alone, whereas group discussions are ideal to evaluate ideas and generate consensus. Idea-generation is just one of many aspects of knowledge work that require quiet, thinking space.

You can still build in lots of opportunities for collaboration. For example:

➤ **Create "coffee house" settings** with comfortable furniture where employees can do low-focus work and mingle (using existing conference rooms or lobbies if an office remodel isn't in the budget).

➤ **Schedule "co-working afternoons" or "collaboration days"** by establishing long stretches of time (a periodic half-day or even full day) when employees are encouraged to bring their laptops and work on lighter tasks away from their office and among their colleagues. Perhaps you can bring in snacks or a meal to make the prospect more enticing to the introverts on your team. More than one of my clients uses this format and brings in beer and wine on Friday afternoons. The goal is still to get work done, but it's an opportunity to save the work that benefits from lots of noise, activity, and collaboration (or at least isn't too harmed by it) until these scheduled times.

➤ **Implement game areas**, which are a great place for collaboration because physical activity fosters imagination. Consider investing in the cost and the space for a foosball table and a Ping-Pong table, for example.

Definitely make collaboration and teamwork a prominent feature of your culture, but don't do it at the expense of the quiet, undistracted environments that support the flow, creativity, and brainpower that are required for the work you hired your knowledge workers to do (and the privacy that will make them happy).

Take a holistic view and feel free to incorporate components that encourage collaboration and transparency, but the general office-space design should prioritize a layout that supports all three types of attention discussed earlier—stimulus-driven, focused, and restorative. Temper any desire for the most open space possible with the recognition that privacy and quiet are also crucial, and the research proving this is clear. Although I don't recommend an open-office floor plan if you are considering changes in your office design, in the next section I do make suggestions that you can use to improve employee well-being and productivity in an open-office setting.

Making an Open Office Work Better

If you decide to proceed with an open floor plan, or you're looking for ways to make an existing open office better serve your employees' needs, simple yet effective solutions can include differing ceiling heights, room dividers, and throw rugs (which can muffle sound). In addition, the following ideas can help:

> *Employees need easy access to quiet, distraction-free environments.*

➤ **Create private spaces:** This is one of the most important ways you can modify an open-office layout to improve productivity. Employees need easy access to quiet, distraction-free environments. Set up areas for individual and small group work. If office space is at a premium, create more private spaces with screens, bookcases, other shelving units, and modular walls.

➤ **Give back some control:** There is evidence that putting workers in charge of office décor, giving them input on common spaces, and letting them totally control their own workspaces can counteract feelings of lost control in an open office.[89] Consider how much input employees will have over the following things:

- Private storage space for snacks, personal articles, and supplies
- Office décor, including personal décor such as family photographs and knickknacks
- Noise, including music or other background sounds
- Lighting
- Temperature
- Personal privacy—for themselves, their belongings, their information, their activities

Here are some ideas to expand on each of these items:

➤ Ease the "fishbowl effect" of glass walls by adding frosted film to create more privacy.

➤ Consider personal desk lamps instead of, or at least in addition to, overhead lighting.

➤ If your office lacks the privacy and quiet needed for deep-focus work, let employees work from home. Telecommuting is the subject of chapter 6, but if working from home is not a good solution, consider augmenting your office space by investing in a low-cost monthly lease at co-working or other hourly office-rental locations, such as WeWork (www.wework.com) or Regus (www.regus.com).

➤ Introduce tools for employees to use to signal they don't want to be interrupted. For example, you can establish a rule that wearing headphones signals "do not disturb" time.

Or you could use red/yellow/green signs, for cubicle walls or the backs of chairs that provide guidance on the type of work each staffer is currently engaged in and how detrimental it might be to be interrupted. You could also engage staff to create entertaining or funny signs for each stage of work (Please do not disturb/red, Disturb if important/yellow, Ok to interrupt/green) and have a set printed for each employee.

➤ With an open-office floor plan, it's especially important to add work-life-management training as discussed in chapter two—that includes "attention management" rather than "time management" as its central theme—to your professional development plans for your team. Managing attention is not something people learn on their own, and I can tell you from my decades in the corporate training industry that your employees are struggling, and it's only getting worse.

➤ Try desks on wheels. Small desks with castors are a minimal investment. Employees gain a sense of control by moving them around as their work—and their mood—dictates.

➤ Ask staff for their input. Talk with your employees about how they would modify your open office to increase productivity. You can use tools such as 15Five (www.15five.com), TINYpulse (www.tinypulse.com), and the Happiness at Work Survey (www.happinessatworksurvey.com) to gather ideas.

➤ Help mitigate background hubbub with white noise. Consider gifting your employees with a subscription to Calm.com, or Focus@Will, (www.focusatwill.com), which both offer audio tracks to support focus, and encouraging use of these services. Another option is to invest in an office sound system and play soothing nature sounds throughout the office. At least one study has suggested that workers' moods and productivity improve when nature sounds are playing in the background.[90]

➤ If your office space is on the first floor (or even if it isn't), try taking advantage of the real estate beyond the walls. Soothing outdoor spaces are conducive to restorative attention time, and can also be used as quiet places to escape for focused work.

➤ If expanding outdoors isn't an option, there are other creative ways of boosting employee well-being and productivity, and mitigating the extra stress an open office can cause. Look for ways of "bringing the outdoors in." Natural light is great, but if you don't have as much access to windows as you would like, or if those windows look out over a man-made landscape instead of nature, you can still reap the benefits with your indoor design by implementing techniques like these:

- Use full-spectrum light bulbs.
- Bring in lots of potted plants.
- Hang pictures of nature scenes or wall-mounted television screens that show outdoor scenes.
- Put a nature slideshow on all company televisions and monitors as screen savers.
- Use nature as the theme for your office décor, and remember that soft furnishings and plants muffle sound, whereas hard surfaces amplify it.

Take Advantage of "Biophilia"

The term *biophilia* is defined as our "urge to affiliate with other forms of life—probably because we evolved to function best in nature-rich settings."[91] Views of nature have been shown to make workers less frustrated, more patient, more productive, and physically healthier.[92]

➤ Consider creating non-work rooms, such as for catnaps. It may seem inappropriate to nap at work, but a ten to twenty minute rest can be among the best antidotes to the mid-afternoon slump, and the best way to tame a wandering mind.[93] In Japan, napping at work is a sign of dedication to the job. Review the information on sleep on page 5 of chapter 1 for all the compelling reasons a nap room will help your employees produce their best work.

➤ Consider standing and treadmill desks, because there is no dispute about the negative health effects of sitting too long, and the positive effects of activity on brainpower and overall wellness. Also like nature and napping, exercise reduces stress.

Influencing Culture

In addition to the floor plan, the behaviors that leadership exhibits have a profound effect on both collaboration and focus. Model, and encourage, single-tasking and restorative attention time. Leaders should actually use the standing or treadmill desks, the outdoor spaces, the nap rooms, and the quiet time. Discourage staff from bringing phones or computers into meetings with them, with the possible exception of the scribe. This will encourage single-tasking and full engagement in the meeting from all the participants.

- -

Conclusion

Open-office floor plans may yet prove to increase collaboration and innovation, but currently, the evidence is still scant. If the financial benefits, in terms of the reduction in real estate, outweigh the disadvantages, you can use the information in this chapter to create an environment that minimizes the square footage required but also supports high-quality knowledge work.

Action Items

These are specific steps that will help you put the information in this chapter to use immediately. Most can be implemented relatively quickly and easily and can pay big returns:

1. If you're designing or redesigning a workspace, consider bucking the open-office trend for the majority of the space, but do incorporate some of the most useful features.

2. Designate different spaces for employees to do different kinds of work, from areas that encourage collaboration to spaces where employees have the privacy, control, and quiet they need to do focused work or to take a restorative break. If you have access to outdoor space, look at its potential to help you provide the areas you need.

3. If you have an open office that lacks distraction-free spaces, try creating them with screens, shelving, and modular walls. You could also allow employees to work from home or in a co-working space.

4. To encourage employees to take advantage of areas for focused work or a restorative break, make sure leaders model this behavior.

5. In an open office, look for ways to give workers back some of the control that this type of layout takes away. They'll feel more in control of their space, for example, if they can make decisions about lighting or décor. Desks on wheels can allow them to change their surroundings when they need to.

6. Allow employees to use signals like wearing headphones or displaying a "do not disturb" sign when they're engaged in focused work.

7. Mitigate background noise: Use a white noise machine or play soothing nature sounds on your office sound system. You could also add more soft surfaces and plants to absorb sound.

8. Add training that incorporates attention management skills so that employees can be more effective amid the distractions of an open office.

9. Get your staff's input on how your workspace can better support their productivity.

- -

Takeaways You Can Tweet

Here are important points of the chapter summarized so that they are easy to digest, but also so that you can conveniently share the information with your followers on Twitter or on other social media outlets. Follow and participate in the conversation online using *#workwithoutwalls*, and/or my handle, @mnthomas.

- ❏ Offices need space for both collaboration and quiet, focused work.

- ❏ Open offices are trendy, but they fail employees in important ways.

- ❏ Open offices take away control. As a leader, think about how to give some back.

- ❏ In an open office, there's less privacy—which may mean less creativity, too.

- ❏ It's not your imagination: Open offices result in more sick time.

- ❏ The efficiency of an office layout isn't just about cost per square foot.

- ❏ To reduce distractions, let employees use headphones and work from home sometimes.

- ❏ Teaching attention management helps employees deal with an open office.

- ❏ One quick way to make an open office calmer: white noise.

- ❏ Adding natural elements can make an open office less stressful.

Chapter 6

THE LOCATION
OF WORK

Telecommuting Is the Future of Work[94]

**—*FORBES* HEADLINE,
JANUARY 12, 2014**

THANKS to new technologies, the barriers to where and when we do work are falling. An example is the rise of telecommuting. Telecommuting is touted as a tool that gives employees—especially parents and caregivers—more flexibility and increased work satisfaction, while saving employers millions of dollars in real estate and office furniture and serving as a recruiting enticement.

There's a lot of hype—and some anxiety—about letting employees work from home instead of at the office. This chapter is intended to give you the information you need to maximize the bene-

Telecommuting means a new way of working and managing, and the transition can be difficult.

fits and minimize the disadvantages of having a telecommuting workforce. Careful consideration, planning, and assessment—along with fully understanding the true issues behind managers' and employees' telecommuting concerns—can help your company clear potential stumbling blocks and reap the benefits of allowing telecommuting.

Telecommuting and Remote Work Are Not the Same

I believe that challenges identified with workers who are outside the traditional office stem at least in part from the failure to distinguish between telecommuting and remote work. I define telecommuting as work done at another location that *replaces* some or all work time that is typically done at the office. In other words, if someone works from home every Tuesday instead of going into the office, that employee is participating in part-time telecommuting.

Work done at a remote location *in addition to* work done at the office is a different thing, which I refer to as remote work. Virtually every professional who uses a smartphone or tablet engages in remote work. The distinction is important because some arguments against "telecommuting"—for example, that it's too easy for work to bleed into personal time—are actually issues related to workplace cultures that encourage 24/7 availability. The complaint is not about the opportunity to replace one workspace for another (telecommuting); it's about the *remote work* that is done—such as incessantly checking email—during time that should be dedicated to personal interests (evenings, weekends, and during vacation). The blurring of the lines between work time and personal time has nothing to do with telecommuting policies; instead, it's a remote work issue, which is discussed in chapter 3.

If your team already engages in remote work, it's hard to make a valid argument against allowing telecommuting. Your employees are currently putting in *more* hours of work from home, after working a full week, so it's unlikely that they would "slack off" as telecommuters simply because there is no one to witness their work time.

Telecommuting Will Only Grow in the Future

I agree with the chapter's introductory quote: Telecommuting is the future of work. A survey by WorldatWork, a nonprofit human resources organization, showed that more than half of organizations offered some type of "regular telework"; although, this is an example of a discussion that does not define the term specifically.[95] I expect that number will only continue to grow. This can put your company at a disadvantage if you don't offer some form of telecommuting.

One reason I believe in the future growth of telecommuting is that the benefits are so numerous, and they span three different areas: social responsibility, individual benefits, and company benefits. Societal issues are often overlooked when considering telecommuting programs, so let's look at those first.

Social Responsibility

Companies with employees who don't have to commute to an office are minimizing environmental cost in terms of reducing traffic and air pollution. Motor vehicles are the biggest contributors to smog, so fewer cars on the road means less yellow haze hanging over your city. It also means fewer traffic jams and traffic fatalities. Telecommuting also reduces the strain on the overtaxed and aging transportation infrastructure in the United States. The American Society of Civil Engineers reports that one in nine of the nation's bridges are rated as structurally deficient, and they give America's overall infrastructure a rating of D+.[96] When more workers telecommute, we are putting less demand on a transportation infrastructure that isn't equipped to tolerate today's load.

In addition, telecommuting can benefit those with physical and other challenges, and those who live in more rural areas, by opening employment opportunities that previously would have been unavailable if those workers had to work at an on-site office location.

Individual Benefits

Employees consider the opportunity to telecommute—replacing in-office hours with hours spent working from home—to be a valuable benefit. The great thing about telecommuting is that employees view it as a benefit, yet it's a perk that can reduce company overhead rather than increase it. Consider these statistics from research by Global Workplace Analytics: [97]

> ➤ Seventy-nine percent of people want to work from home.
> ➤ Thirty-nine percent would choose the opportunity to telecommute over a pay raise.

89

> Sixty-one percent of employees who do not currently work from home say they are willing to give up some pay in order to do so.

> Eighty percent of employees consider telework a job perk.

Employees can have better work-life balance because they reclaim the time they spend "getting ready" and commuting and use the time to pursue activities that benefit them personally, such as getting more sleep, eating better, engaging in hobbies, and spending more time with family. Employees' expenses also decrease when they work from home, which means they have more income without receiving a raise. Travel expenses—such as gas, insurance, and maintenance—decrease, and if the family can drop down to one car, there's also a decrease in auto loan expenses. Also, employees can invest less in their wardrobes when they don't need to dress up for work and aren't seeing the same people every day.

Chapter 1 illustrates how these improvements to holistic employee wellness also benefit the organization.

Other benefits of telecommuting for the individual, which also benefit the organization, include the opportunity to deal better with family issues, personal needs, illness, and stress, and telecommuters are exposed to fewer airborne illnesses. Cumulatively, these things reduce the amount of sick time used. Employees are also better able to attend to personal appointments and errands without missing a full day of work. Lastly, the solitude and seclusion of working from home is a big advantage to telecommuters who would otherwise work in an open area or cubicle and consequently feel a loss of their privacy.

Company Benefits

Many of the benefits related to social responsibility and individuals also benefit organizations by indirectly reducing costs and increasing productivity. The following are some direct improvements to productivity and the bottom line, according to Global Workplace Analytics: [98]

> More than two-thirds of employers report increased productivity among their telecommuters.

> Forty-six percent of companies that allow telecommuting say it has reduced attrition.

> ➤ Telecommuters tend to put in more hours for the organization.

> ➤ Employers see direct cost reductions in the following areas:

- Real estate
- Office equipment
- ADA compliance expenses
- Relocation expenses

Knowledge worker productivity is addressed in chapter 7, but my study has led me to the conclusion that the measurement of knowledge work must be based on a combination of outputs, outcomes, and job satisfaction. Telecommuting requires measurement beyond what can be observed in an office setting and, therefore, provides incentives to find more objective, and results-based, performance measurements, which benefits the organization in the long run.

Lastly, when organizations are unconstrained by geographic location, they can expand the pool from which talent is drawn. This aspect of telecommuting will be increasingly important as the job market and the race for talent continue to become more and more competitive.

Challenges to Consider

Transitioning to working in and managing a telecommuting environment isn't always smooth. Some managers believe that, at best, employees will be too distracted by personal tasks and issues if allowed to work remotely, and, at worst, employees will slack off if they aren't directly supervised. Employees who telecommute instead of working at the office may worry that they'll be overlooked and not recognized because they're not as visible to managers as their in-house peers. It's also true that work can bleed into personal time, creating an "always-on" environment in which there is no time to relax, recharge, and unplug.[99]

"In-Person" Time Does Have Benefits

Although it's hardly the norm, a growing number of businesses are organized with a 100 percent distributed workforce, meaning that there is no "home office" or company-leased real estate. Given the increase in teams operating from disparate locations, it's useful to itemize some benefits of having in-person time that can be neglected in situations with 100 percent telecommuting. The following are four of those benefits:

> **Building trust:** It's difficult to get to know people, and therefore to trust them, when you are never in the same physical location. Often, we begin building trust with someone by shaking hands when we first meet. This touch, and other casual interaction that occurs when we meet face-to-face in professional situations, primes the brain to release chemicals associated with trust and empathy.[100] Therefore, people who see each other in person frequently can find it easier to form trusting relationships.

> **Clarity of communication:** Another advantage of in-person interaction is that meaning is easier to discern in person. Facial expressions and other body language, tone, inflection, and attitude are all important components of communication, much more important than words alone. Therefore, meaning can be lost or misunderstood when communication is primarily written. Clarity is critical to efficiency and productivity, and emoticons can only take you so far in conveying the subtle nuances of communication! Attention is another necessary ingredient for clarity, and you are more likely to have someone's full attention when she can see you.

> **Using visual cues:** Visual cues with regard to body language help direct a dialogue and are often used as turning points in the conversation: when you notice someone's eyes drifting away, it could mean that he is losing interest in the conversation, and depending on the nature of the discussion, you know it's time to move on, bring the conversation to a close, or change your approach. On the other hand, when someone leans forward in her seat, she is likely highly engaged and giving you positive cues about her level of engagement and your approach. These types of visual cues

are impossible in written communication or even over the phone.

> **Creating camaraderie:** Telecommuters can easily feel disconnected and isolated, especially when they're geographically distant and rarely, if ever, come into the office. In-person time fosters community and reminds employees that they are involved in something bigger than themselves.

These four components help create rapport, and rapport builds relationships. When you work with a telecommuting team, some of these issues can be overcome with video calls, but video calls don't fully compensate for these deficiencies. Therefore, companies that are 100 percent distributed should be thoughtful about addressing these issues. The following are some ways to bring the benefits of in-person communication to a 100 percent distributed team:

> Use group video calls, such as Google Hangouts (hangouts. google.com), which allow up to ten people to participate at once, and ensure all telecommuters have access to an Internet connection that can support high-quality video calls.

See appendix C for a detailed list of all tools, apps, websites, and other resources mentioned throughout this book.

> Ensure that all employees have, and are properly trained on using, a video call service, such as Skype (www.skype.com).

> Set the tone, as the leader, by using video calls instead of phone whenever possible, and encourage employees to use video calls so that the practice is embedded into the culture of the organization.

> Add a line item to the budget for annual (or more frequent, if possible) team get-togethers. If there are staff who are within a few hours' drive of each other, encourage them to get together more often by renting co-working space for them to meet, or simply co-work, periodically.

Distraction

Managers who are used to having employees close at hand in the office may worry that staffers who work at home will be too distracted by personal concerns, which will affect the employees' ability to be productive. This fear is due to the fact that productivity is hard to measure in knowledge work, so managers often rely on their ability to see a worker sitting at a desk and working. However, this concern is an outdated management bias and is unreliable for many reasons, not the least of which is that knowledge work is the result of intangibles like creativity and thinking, which are hard to observe.

Granted, employees who work remotely experience distractions, but it's a mistake to think that distraction is uniquely a telecommuting problem. Most work settings have distractions. Think of all the overheard conversations and interruptions in an office with an open floor plan. Chapter 5 discusses some disadvantages of open floor plans, and telecommuting can alleviate or reduce some of those detrimental issues. Wherever knowledge workers are doing their jobs—home, office, coffee shop, hotel room—they deal with the barrage of information from all their electronic devices and their own difficulties with focus. The true issue isn't where employees work; it's whether they know how to manage their attention.

Another reason the attention management training discussed in chapter 2 is so important.

Work-Life Balance: Are Telecommuters Really "Always On"?

Telecommuting naysayers often point to studies showing that employees who work at home instead of in the office put in more hours. These studies argue that employees who telecommute will find work intruding more and more on their personal lives.

If we are careful to emphasize the distinction between telecommuting and remote work that I described on page 88, then I believe either group is just as likely to engage in work after hours.

> *It's a mistake to think that distraction is uniquely a telecommuting problem.*

When a company's telecommuters find themselves working longer hours and blurring the boundaries between work and home life, it's likely the result of the same assumptions and difficulties that all employees face, which are described in chapter 3:

➤ Feeling overwhelmed by email and other communication, due to inadequate workflow-management skills

➤ Having unrealistic expectations about what can be accomplished in a day

➤ Having poor attention-management skills

➤ Improperly using communication tools

➤ Lacking understanding of expectations and policies, which are often undefined and unclear

➤ Following leaders who have ineffective habits

➤ Allowing ambition to drive their desire to be seen as exceptionally responsive

➤ Experiencing telepressure ◄

Telepressure is defined on page 50 of chapter 3.

Another issue at play, which is specific to telecommuters, is that the employees may believe that their managers don't trust and don't know how to lead employees they can't directly observe. Worried that they will be overlooked or evaluated poorly, employees try to "make up for" their lack of physical presence in the office by working longer hours and being always available via email.

The two challenges discussed thus far—distraction and work-life balance—may signal problems in the workplace culture that go beyond issues with telecommuting. For example, managers might have outdated ideas about how to lead and evaluate in the world of work without walls. Physical presence in the office isn't the best indicator of the engagement and creativity that knowledge work depends on.

It's important to remember that a detrimental always-on environment isn't about the location of the work; it's about workplace culture and whether that culture is intentional (in other

> *Physical presence in the office isn't the best indicator of the engagement and creativity that knowledge work depends on.*

words, created with forethought by leadership) or is the unintended by-product of employee assumptions, habits, and behaviors (which is the more common situation).

Defining Work-Life Balance

The idea of "work-life balance" comes up frequently in discussions about telecommuting. It's a subjective concept. I discuss it in depth in chapter 1, where I define *balance* as a life that includes activities that not only nurture professional desires and personal pursuits but also puts an intentional focus on all aspects of well-being, contentment, and satisfaction, such as healthy introspection and analysis, strong social ties, hobbies, personal growth, and financial sustainability. Furthermore, work-life balance is simply the ability to be *present* in whatever you are attending to: immersed in your professional life when working, and fully engaged in family, leisure, or recreation activities when you're not working. Also, in the context of employee wellness, a relevant proverb reminds us that, "Health is not merely the absence of disease but the balance of mind, body, and soul."

Security

Data security is an increasing concern in this age of cyberfraud. A number of my clients have fallen prey to a scheme that involves spoofing the email address of a C-level executive in which a bogus message is sent to the accounts payable department requesting a wire transfer. The money is seldom recovered, and the perpetrators are often impossible to prosecute. When employees rarely see each other and rely heavily on email and other indirect communication tools, companies are especially vulnerable to this type of scam.

A report from Ernst & Young and the Center for Democracy & Technology outlined a number of challenges to data security inside organizations:[101]

> ➤ Cybersecurity concerns for telecommuters are often side-lined while the company attends to more immediate data-breach issues.

➤ Telecommuting issues cut across departmental boundaries, so there is a lack of clear ownership of responsibility for data security issues with regard to telecommuters.

➤ Because telecommuting practices often evolve organically, no formal procedures or training on data security exist at most organizations.

➤ Background screening of contractors and employees who telecommute is inconsistent.

➤ Protections are implemented for technology used by telecommuters, but there are few safeguards and rules regarding paper generated by telecommuters.

➤ Privacy-enhancing technologies are slow to take hold, and practices with regard to portable devices is lacking.

Despite these challenges, I recommend that some opportunity for employees to replace in-office work time with at-home work time be implemented in most every organization. Insisting that all work be done at a corporate office is, in most cases, an outdated practice. Telecommuting offers numerous benefits to the organization, is preferred by employees, and is better for society and the environment.

Institutional Changes: Making Telecommuting Work for Your Company

As with other productivity factors, what's important about telecommuting policies and practices is that they are crafted and implemented with intention. When they emerge organically over time, the organization can be subject to security issues, the impression of favoritism, disconnected teams, and employee burnout. The suggestions discussed next will help you reap the benefits and avoid the drawbacks.

Evaluating Whether an Employee Is Ready to Telecommute

Ask yourself the following questions to evaluate whether a specific employee should be allowed to replace all or part of his or her time working in the office with telecommuting:

➤ *What is the employee's job role? How much of the work is solitary versus group? How collaborative is the role?* Even collaborative roles have components more suited to solitary work. But more collaborative roles might be better suited to more in-office time. See the sidebar below for the way American Express relates the job role to the location where the work gets done.

At Amex, Where You Work Depends on What You Do

When considering replacing in-office hours with off-site hours, an important factor in the decision making is the type of job being done. American Express is having great success with its BlueWork program, which uses an employee survey to designate jobs as Hub (full-time in office), Club (part-time in office), Home (full-time home office), or Roam ("road warriors" without an office).[102] The nature of the job drives the decision about the necessary workspace.

➤ *What kind of productivity habits does the employee have?* Strong productivity habits are a good sign that an employee will succeed with telecommuting. Here are some examples of qualities to look for:

- Possessing a system for managing all details of life and work, including a calendar and a well-prioritized to-do list. (Paper is okay, but embracing technology is important for telecommuters.)
- Working reasonable hours.
- Meeting deadlines.
- Having a positive (motivated and energized) attitude toward work rather than an overwhelmed, exhausted perspective.
- Possessing strong attention-management skills: exhibiting control over distractions, usually single-tasking instead of

multitasking, and employing sustained (focused) attention when necessary. Exhibiting control over technology rather than letting days be dictated by incoming communication. (As mentioned in chapter 3, attention management is an emerging skill, and it can be taught.)

➤ *How proficient are the employee's tech skills?*
Technology must play a big part in the workday of telecommuters. Does the employee have the following skills?

- Proficient with technology in general.

- Fluent in your company's specific tools for telecommuters.

- Able to learn the necessary technologies. A new telecommuter fresh from a traditional office with support services at the ready may have to be taught simple tricks to independently solve problems—for example, doing an Internet search for a technical issue before contacting tech support.

➤ *What will the employee's telework setup be?*
Just as your office's environment affects productivity there, the employee's work-at-home setup affects productivity when telecommuting. The company needs to provide someone who will assess the employee's workspace for the following things:

- A dedicated workspace (Chances are, a corner of the dining table isn't very conducive to quality work.)

- A fast and reliable Internet connection

- Other family members (especially children or others needing care) present during work hours

- Training and demonstrated techniques, technology, and office equipment for handling privacy, confidentiality, and security issues

Read more about this in "Why Your Workspace Matters to Your Productivity at www.regain-yourtime.com/why-your-work-space-matters-to-your-productivity/.

Create a Safe and Productive Culture for Telecommuting

To make telecommuting work for your company, it's important to assess the attitudes, readiness, and capabilities of your employees, your managers, and the company as a whole. These steps will help you do a thorough assessment.

Talk to your employees. Would they like to have the option to telecommute if it doesn't already exist? If it does exist, how do they feel it's working? How is telecommuting (or its absence, if your company doesn't allow it) affecting morale, retention, and hiring? What other attitudes and opinions do your employees have about telecommuting?

Look at telecommuting policies. Using ideas from American Express, decide which roles are well suited to telework. Consider which employees will be offered the opportunity to telecommute. Identify what limitations, if any, you will set. If the option won't be available to everyone, try to predict how that will affect morale. Decide who on the leadership team will oversee telecommuting policies, and determine whether that person has the skills and experience to do so effectively.

Get Ahead of Legislation

England has given workers more control over when and where they work by implementing legislation guaranteeing employees the right to ask for flexibility, such as the opportunity to telecommute. Employers can deny the request, but they must provide a reason, and workers can appeal the decision. According to University of Texas sociologist and telecommuting expert Jennifer Glass, "Most requests don't seem to disturb the workplace, and it hasn't clogged the courts there."[103]

Examine your managers' attitudes. Managers who have the outdated bias that employees must be supervised in order to be productive should have a skill update. To effectively manage telecommuters, supervisors must believe—unless they have evidence to the contrary—that people are working even if they are not in the office. Supervisors also need tools and training to efficiently track telework and to avoid micro-managing telecommuting employees. Use the following questions as a guide:

- Will supervisors embrace their staff working off-site instead of at the office?

- Are there tools in place—other than direct observation—to assess work performance?

- Can you detect any unspoken biases toward telecommuting?

- Does your company have adequate feedback mechanisms for all sides involved with telecommuting, including mechanisms for both formal and informal reviews and for identified and anonymous feedback? Or are employee performance and engagement assessments left to subjective opinions and isolated anecdotes?

Assessing Performance with Technology

Employee-monitoring software is an option that has received a bad reputation that was earned by being used punitively. Keystroke software is viewed as spying on employees, and it's seen as a sign of mistrust, which can negatively infect the culture of an organization. However, new iterations of this software, such as the offering from Sapience (www.sapience.net), can be implemented transparently and embraced by the employees if the goals of the organization are truly benign and altruistic and employed for the benefit of employees and the greater good of the organization. Some advantages of this type of software include:

- Enhancing the ability for employees to understand how they spend their time and consequently improve their productivity

- Providing options to reclaim productive time when inefficiencies are uncovered, thereby potentially reducing work hours and achieving better work-life balance

- Allowing unbiased performance indicators

- Addressing security concerns

- Capturing best practices from high performers

- Understanding appropriate ramp-up time and training needs for new employees.

In the wrong hands, though, and with the wrong motives, this type of technology still has the potential to undermine trust and erode goodwill in the corporate culture. If you are considering such an employee-monitoring tool at your organization, I recommend rolling it out in a completely transparent way and allowing employees to initially keep their use data private, for their own personal evaluation. Later, metrics can be offered in aggregate, so as not to unfairly target specific employees, and employees should always know that their computer use is being monitored. Also, the benefit of the doubt is important for maintaining trust. Don't let managers jump to conclusions about employees with unfavorable metrics, because there are many benign reasons for unfavorable metrics, including: a need for more training; a technology malfunction, such as slow-running computers; and an honest misunderstanding about goals and priorities. Monitoring software can add valuable data that leads to individual and corporate benefits when used appropriately. However, it can also lead to suspicion, mistrust, and an erosion of corporate culture when mishandled.

Assess your tech tools. Employees who replace some or all of their in-office time with tele-commuting will use an array of technology to connect with colleagues. Also, your company's confidential data must be a concern. You can help telework go more smoothly by looking at questions like these:

> *To effectively manage telecommuters, supervisors must believe—unless they have evidence to the contrary—that people are working even if they are not in the office.*

- Is the company using tools that support telework? These tools can include video calls, VPN, company bulletin boards and wikis, online collaborative tools, social media platforms, etc.

- If so, are these tools being used effectively? For example, are there policies or understandings about which tools to use in which circumstances? When new tools are introduced with no policy or plan, the result is an unnecessary increase in internal communication.

- Do employees know where different information lives? You don't want them to waste time searching the shared hard drive, intranet, etc., for the information they need.

- If you use an instant messenger tool, are there best practices in place that employees know about? Is it acceptable, for example, to set one's status to "away"? If so, how often?

- Has the staff received training on your tech tools?

- Are all employees using the tools, and are they using them appropriately?

- Does the IT department spend an excessive amount of time supporting these tools?

Combat isolation. Telecommuters should have frequent and regular video calls with supervisors and their larger team. Offer them the opportunity to visit the office with some regularity. Local employees should visit the office at least once per week. Allocate financial resources so that regional telecommuters can visit and work in-house monthly or quarterly, national employees quarterly or biannually, and international employees at least annually. Try to have an "all team" event at least once per year for everyone to get together for professional development and also social activities.

Take cybersecurity seriously. Failure to have protection against data breaches introduces risk to the company's corporate reputation, regulatory compliance, and data in terms of data corruption and misuse. Safeguards intended for telecommuters will increase the data security of the entire organization and minimize risks across all departments. A report from Ernst & Young/CDT offers a comprehensive guide, including these suggestions:[104]

- Provide telecommuters with shredders and locked cabinets.
- Have periodic inspections of telework environments.
- Limit the use of external memory devices.
- Use encryption to connect to internal networks.

Although I recommend it, there are many issues to consider when implementing a telecommuting policy—so many that without careful consideration, important issues can be neglected. This is another reason that you shouldn't allow your telecommuting policy to evolve organically but rather create it with intention.

- -

Conclusion

Allowing employees to telecommute rather than working on-site opens your company up to being able to recruit talent globally. That's alluring, especially if your local market has a dearth of top talent. But as you make plans for addressing the issues raised in this chapter, consider including a trial period in your plans, even for employees who would telecommute only part-time. And try telecommuting with local employees before you hire nonlocal telecommuters. These trials will give you the ability to fully understand the issues, learn how telecommuting will be received at the organization, and prepare you to address the situations that arise.

- -

Action Items

These are specific steps that will help you put the information in this chapter to use immediately. Most can be implemented relatively quickly and easily and can pay big returns:

1. If the members of your team work from separate locations, have meetings using video calls whenever possible to enhance communication and trust.
2. For regional employees within driving distance of each other, plan get-togethers and encourage them to meet up or co-work regularly.

3. Budget for telecommuters to visit the office as frequently as makes sense for their location. Workers in the region could visit monthly or quarterly, while international workers might be on an annual schedule.

4. To decide whether an employee can work from home instead of at the office, use the criteria in this chapter, including the employee's role and productivity habits.

5. Meet with leadership to evaluate your current telecommuting policy. Which workers can telecommute? Do you place any limits on telecommuting? Who oversees and updates your policies?

6. Get input from your employees about how your telecommuting policy (or lack of one) affects them.

7. Add to your one-on-one meeting agenda with your managers a discussion regarding their management of telecommuters. Are their attitudes outdated? Give supervisors tools and training to efficiently track work done off-site and to avoid micromanaging telecommuters.

8. Ask your telecommuters: is all technology you use adequate to support your work? Ask your IT team (or get specialized help if you need it) to ensure company data is secure for telecommuters.

9. See how telecommuting works with local employees before you hire nonlocal telecommuters.

💬 Takeaways You Can Tweet

Here are important points of the chapter summarized so that they are easy to digest, but also so that you can conveniently share the information with your followers on Twitter or on other social media outlets. Follow and participate in the conversation online using *#workwithout-walls,* and/or my handle, @mnthomas.

❏ It's a mistake to think that distraction is uniquely a telecommuting problem.

- ❏ Remote work adds work time. Telecommuting replaces time in the office. When considering issues, don't confuse them.

- ❏ The best way to judge employees' creativity and engagement ISN'T whether they're physically in the office.

- ❏ Setting telecommuters up for success takes planning.

- ❏ If work bleeds over into telecommuters' personal time, that's a culture issue not a telecommuting issue.

- ❏ Use video conferencing with telecommuters. It's closer to in-person communication.

- ❏ Encourage your telecommuters to get together or even work together sometimes.

- ❏ When your company allows telecommuting, you're doing social good.

- ❏ Win-win: Employees want telecommuting, and it saves companies money.

- ❏ Telecommuting can help build morale and fight attrition.

- ❏ Telecommuters (and all workers) must know how to manage their attention.

- ❏ Before saying 'you can work from home,' examine employee's role, productivity habits, tech skills.

- ❏ Try telecommuting with local employees before hiring nonlocal telecommuters.

- ❏ Get employee feedback on telecommuting and examine your policies.

- ❏ Do your managers have outmoded attitudes on telecommuting? Help them get up to date.

- ❏ Make sure your company's tech both supports telecommuters and protects your data.

- ❏ Telecommuters should still visit the office sometimes.

Chapter 7

INTENTION AND IMPROVEMENT

The most valuable asset of a 21st-century institution (whether business or non-business) will be its knowledge workers and their productivity.[105]

—**PETER F. DRUCKER**

THERE is common agreement, from Peter Drucker to McKinsey & Company and to me, that the shift from industrial and agricultural work to knowledge work without walls poses a challenge for measuring—and therefore improving—productivity. Part of that challenge is leaving behind notions about what constitutes productivity — such as constant availability, face time at the office, and even a certain pride in working at a relentless pace—that we now know are detrimental and unsustainable.

Business leaders throughout corporate America will continue to face this challenge for the foreseeable future, especially because the meaning of *productivity* will vary among organizations and industries. No matter their field, though, forward-thinking businesses can position themselves to thrive by embracing the truth that knowledge workers' productivity is dependent upon factors that aren't often considered, such as their well-being and state of mind, their work environment, and their opportunities for downtime. With the suggestions from this book, and specifically this chapter, it's possible for leaders to gain increased insight on the current state of their organization's productivity and to begin taking the steps that will lead to improvement.

Productivity Requires Intention

One thing should be clear by now: In order to improve individual and organizational productivity, intention is necessary. The issues discussed in this book are reshaping the modern workplace. You and your leadership team must recognize and identify company behaviors and practices that may have evolved by chance, consider them carefully, and then thoughtfully design your policies and plans with intention. This will maximize your benefits and avoid serious negative consequences including lawsuits, difficulty hiring, and loss of competitive advantage.

Great results don't "just happen," and in this new world of work without walls, you can't leave productivity to chance. Attention—or the lack thereof—to productivity issues can make or break a corporate culture, so leaders have to be deliberate about establishing and nurturing a culture that supports knowledge workers' productivity.

Focusing specific intention on knowledge worker productivity is especially important because today's workplace is more complex, with more demands on your employees' attention. Knowledge workers are constantly distracted by technology and their own inattentiveness, and they're at more risk than ever of being always busy but never productive. The important work that moves individual and corporate goals forward requires intellectual resources in the form of creativity, inspiration, and insight, and that's rarely the kind of work that lives in email or that can be done in two-minute increments. High-quality knowledge work requires workers' full attention, for longer periods of time than the typical two- or five-minute bursts between task-switching.

Examine the Cost of Old Habits

Individual habits shape corporate culture, yet my twenty-plus years of working in the productivity industry have shown me that the current habits of employees—even successful employees—are no longer sufficient for the new realities of the business world, and the skills gap is leaving knowledge workers exhausted. Not only are these outdated habits bad for employees and the work they produce, but they also cost organizations billions of dollars in productivity loss.

Here's an example of a bad habit that might be adversely affecting productivity: In chapter 2, I discuss that I have observed that most employees leave their email clients open all the time. New messages arrive, with some sort of alert or indication, every 30 to 120 seconds, disrupting focus. I encourage you to observe your employees to see if this behavior is common in your office. These are just anecdotal observations, though, so let's examine the results of an empirical study.

Professor Gloria Mark at the University of California, Irvine, has conducted research that shows the average worker is interrupted every eleven minutes,[106] and it takes twenty-three minutes and fifteen seconds[107] to recover from the distraction. In financial terms, if the average salary at your organization is $50,000 per year, then each 23.25-minute distraction costs $9.69 (See Figure 7.1 on next page). Multiply that cost by the number of distractions the average employee experiences per day, times the days worked in a year, times the number of employees in an organization, and think about the overall effect on the bottom line of your organization. If your company has fifty-five employees, Mark's research says that the cost of just one distraction per hour, per employee is over a million dollars annually in lost productivity (see Figure 7.1 on next page).

When you take it a step further and multiply your company's results by the number of organizations in the United States, you can see that we experience billions of dollars annually in lost productivity as a nation.

One way to relieve some of this loss of productivity is for leaders to be mindful of habits and environments related to multitasking, communication, and distraction and to ensure that the individuals, leadership, and the entire corporate culture support productivity and attention rather than sabotaging it.

THE COSTS OF DISTRACTION

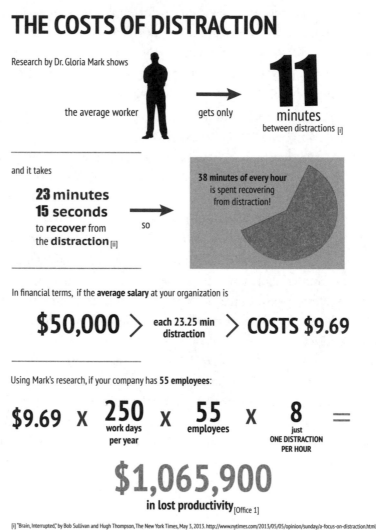

Research by Dr. Gloria Mark shows

the average worker → gets only **11** minutes between distractions [i]

and it takes

23 minutes
15 seconds
to **recover** from the **distraction** [ii]

SO →

38 minutes of every hour is spent recovering from distraction!

In financial terms, if the **average salary** at your organization is

$50,000 〉 each 23.25 min distraction 〉 **COSTS $9.69**

Using Mark's research, if your company has **55 employees**:

$9.69 X **250** work days per year X **55** employees X **8** just ONE DISTRACTION PER HOUR =

$1,065,900
in lost productivity [Office 1]

[i] "Brain, Interrupted," by Bob Sullivan and Hugh Thompson, The New York Times, May 3, 2013. http://www.nytimes.com/2013/05/05/opinion/sunday/a-focus-on-distraction.html

[ii] "Worker, Interrupted: The Cost of Task Switching," by Kermit Pattison, Fast Company, July 28, 2008. http://www.fastcompany.com/944128/worker-interrupted-cost-task-switching

[Office1]Margin note: 1 distraction/hr X 8 hrs/day X 50 employees X 5 days/week X 50 weeks/year X $9.69/distraction = $969,000

Figure 7.1. *Cost of Distraction.*

Look for Signs of an Unintentional Culture

If any of the issues discussed in previous chapters exist at your company, you have an opportunity to enact change. Direct the attention of appropriate leadership toward the issues, take stock of the impact the issues have on productivity and the company's success, and identify and encourage behavior and policy changes with the goal of improvement. Use these questions (recapped from the previous chapters) as you look for signs of an unintentional culture in your organization:

- Is attention given to employees' well-being? Is there a gap in any wellness and engagement initiatives you might be undertaking?

- Is distraction recognized as a threat to productivity, or is it accepted as a routine characteristic of the office?

- Are workflow-management skills lacking at the organization, is training planned to address this need, and are the current training offerings (especially with regard to "time management") adequate to address the new realities of work?

- Is email communication efficient at your organization, or is it dysfunctional—rife with after-hours communication, immediate responses, constant monitoring, and other detrimental habits?

- Are attitudes and behaviors with regard to vacations and downtime supporting or sabotaging quality knowledge work?

- Have you considered how employee's physical workspace (whether they work at the office or at home) affects individual and corporate productivity?

- Are managers equipped to manage knowledge workers, regardless of where they work?

- Are employees cleared to work at home instead of at the office without someone identifying and assessing the technology skills, work environment, and productivity habits they need to succeed?

Create Your Culture with Intention

A good starting point for creating an intentional culture is to use the "Institutional Changes" and "Action Items" sections in each chapter to begin to address the issues in your organization. Consider putting one member of leadership in charge of addressing one or more of each of the subjects covered in this book. First, though, those leaders have to assess and improve their own behaviors, because the message to employees is strongest when leaders model productive behaviors. Regardless of the area being targeted for improvement, the following steps will be useful:

1. *Identify misalignment between your culture and your stated beliefs.* Do your current

> **You'll send the strongest message when leaders model productive behaviors.**

mission and vision take knowledge worker productivity into account? How do your beliefs, values, and goals specifically address maximizing the quality of your outputs? It's important in this conversation to unearth conflicting impressions that have been holding back your productivity culture. For example:

    a. You may identify that your organizational values include creativity and innovation, but there's a persistence of habits and practices that keep employees tethered to email; prevent them from recharging their wells of fresh thinking; and cause them to work in noisy, distracted environments, which are all characteristics that are directly conflicting with your stated values.

    b. You may believe that quality of work is what matters, but perhaps you have managers who are evaluating employees according to whether they're "always on" without considering how their work performances are affecting the rest of their lives. Or you may have managers who are overlooking the contributions of those who work at home just because they're not getting "face time."

2. *Set policies and best practices.* Use the conclusions drawn from Step 1 to shape your productivity policies and practices. Getting everyone on the same page is important. For example, when you have guidelines for managers on how to evaluate employees who work at home, you avoid inconsistent treatment. When you establish that you want employees to have time away from email to do focused work, or more time away from work to recharge and refresh, you may decide to change communication practices, introduce policies like "zmail," discussed in chapter 3, or implement technology tools like scheduled sends and/or auto-deletes combined with auto-responders.

3. *Get the word out and model the behaviors you want to see.* The organizational culture starts at the top, so it's important for leadership to be fully committed to making changes. In addition, the new values and behaviors should be explicitly stated as well as being modeled by leadership. If, for example, you're trying to change an environment where employees have felt uncomfortable about using all their vacation days, they'll feel more secure about taking time off when they've been encouraged to do so and they see leaders doing it.

4. *Equip employees with the skills they need to succeed in the world of work without walls.* Being productive amid all the distractions and complexities of the twenty-first-century office isn't intuitive. The necessary skills are not taught in school or in traditional productivity training—which focuses on time management— and the underlying environment seems to evolve organically without intention as an incremental result of the rapid technology changes. Offering your employees updated productivity training, with a focus on attention management, will help them be more productive, engaged, and happy. Leadership training on creating an environment conducive to productive knowledge work will also ensure improved personal productivity and organizational productivity.

Learn more about training on the concepts in this book by visiting www.regainyourtime.com.

Improving Significant Results

"Improving productivity" sounds like a great idea for anyone, but in order to do this, you first have to get specific about what it means. For my work with my clients, I define productivity as achieving "significant" results. *Significant*, of course, is subjective; for personal productivity, the worker defines the significance. For corporate productivity, the leadership defines the significance. In general, though, if being productive means "achieving significant results," then "improving productivity" means improving results.

Production work in the industrial and agricultural sectors produces outputs, which are based on some predetermined, objective, minimum level of quality and are clearly quantifiable. Examples are the number of units produced or the yield of a crop harvested. Results of productivity are easy to measure.

In knowledge work, we can improve results quantitatively by increasing or decreasing some objective number, such as serving more customers or processing fewer product returns. We can also improve results qualitatively, which is a subjective measure of some intangible aspect of the work, such as writing more engaging articles or devising a more creative marketing strategy. This subjective measure is guided by desired outcomes.

Knowledge workers produce both out*puts* and out*comes.*

Outputs versus Outcomes in Knowledge Work

Knowledge worker *outputs* include decisions, information, and communications. The outputs can be quantified, but the quantity is less relevant than the quality. For example, if a salesperson produces five customer proposals one week and ten customer proposals the next week but closes none of them, then productivity hasn't improved.

Quality is harder to measure. According to management guru Peter Drucker, the quality of an output can be determined only by first identifying the desired outcome.[108] *Outcomes* are the ultimate goal of the outputs. Using the sales example mentioned earlier, the desired outcome of proposals could be more sales or, more generally, increased revenue.

A salesperson who improves his ability to understand a client's needs might write "better" proposals that result in more sales. After you have defined "quality," you can understand how to improve the results—the productivity.

Let's examine the sales example more closely. At first it seems relatively easy to quantify outcomes: more sales closed. But if we try to define the outcome more specifically, it quickly becomes apparent that *quality* is harder to determine. How, exactly, do you determine the quality of a sale?

➤ Are all sales equal, so more of any kind of sale would be a productivity improvement?

➤ If not, what defines a "good" sale?

- High profit margin?
- Longevity of the customer?
- Profile of the customer? (Is a sale to a high-profile customer more valuable than a sale to someone else? To answer this, think about whether it might matter to your business if your client list is composed of recognizable names versus unknown names.)
- Ease of doing business with a customer? (For example, someone who is easy to satisfy and takes very little time to manage rather than someone who has very high expectations and is always demanding more.)

When you've specifically defined the outcome (not only more sales, but the quality of the sale—more of a particular kind of sale, to a particular kind of customer), then you have an understanding of how to increase your salesperson's productivity by closing more of *that type* of sale.

It is easier to specifically address the quality of outcome in some types of knowledge work than in others. For example, can you easily name your specific desired outcome for your operations manager? Would your operations manager give the exact same answer? Even when it's difficult to define the desired outcome for a particular position, you need to take the time to do it for your key knowledge workers in order to define improvement for those positions.

Inputs of Knowledge Work

Once you know the productivity outcomes you'd like to see, then the next step is to make changes to the factors that affect productivity (the inputs) to support those results. In the sales example, what affects your salesperson's ability to make more of what you consider to be "quality" sales?

All the ideas in this book discuss inputs and how to produce maximum results from those inputs. To recap:

➤ Holistic wellness for the proper functioning of the raw material (brain power) for knowledge work and the outputs of this raw material: decisions, ideas, communications, and information

➤ Distraction and attention

➤ Workflow-management processes

➤ Effective communication, specifically with regard to email

➤ Vacation, downtime, and proper rest

➤ The environments where the work is produced

Not only should you go through this exercise for your employees' roles, but you should also do it for the goals of your entire business. Consider an example from Peter Drucker: One pharmaceutical company defines its specific desired outcome as avoiding failures—that is, in "working steadily on fairly minor but predictable improvements in existing products and for established markets." Another pharmaceutical company defines its specific desired outcome as "producing 'breakthroughs'"; consequently, that company courts risks. Each company defines its desired results differently, and therefore each would use a different approach to improving inputs.[109]

The crux of the situation is that when it comes to improving knowledge work, you must first assess the specific desired outcomes. The challenge is that intangible qualitative factors, with no obvious return on investment—such as how an employee feels about her job, the mood he's in on a given day, or the amount of sleep she got the night before—are important components of achieving those outcomes.

However, when these intangible, qualitative productivity components are considered, addressed, and modeled with specific intention, the results are always better than when those components are left to chance.

Institutional Changes: Productivity, Happiness, and Return on Investment

On the surface, the topics in this book are corporate issues that influence productivity; what might be less obvious is that these same issues also influence employee happiness. In corporate America, happiness and productivity are almost synonymous. As previously mentioned, knowledge worker productivity is based on outcomes that result directly and indirectly from the brain (the physical functioning of the tangible organ) and the mind (the intangible outputs of brain functioning including feelings, thoughts, imagination, beliefs, and attitudes). As a result, productivity in knowledge work should be taken out of the realm of quantifiable outputs and moved into the category of qualitative outcomes: creativity, positivity, inspiration, motivation—all of which improve when employees are happier.

Harvard professor and "happiness expert" Shawn Achor reminds us that happiness (also referred to as a positive mind-set) is not a result of success; instead happiness *creates* success. He calls this the 'happiness advantage'—every business outcome shows improvement when the brain is positive,[110] so improving productivity (and happiness) adds value to the bottom line.

Improving Knowledge Worker Productivity

I have seen firsthand how attending to these issues directly and indirectly improves results throughout organizations. My clients are knowledge workers, and in the corporate productivity trainings I deliver, I equip employees to increase their personal productivity by giving them the tools to effectively manage their workflow and their attention, and to maximize their knowledge work outcomes by improving their inputs. My attendees learn how things like well-being, noise, distraction, privacy, and other inputs affect their outcomes, including decisions, communications, creativity, and ideas.

The personal benefits to these employees are quickly apparent. "Life-changing" is the most common phrase I hear to describe effects of the training. But the effect of the training reaches beyond the personal level; these personal benefits indirectly affect the organization. Ninety-day post-training surveys show that 94.6 percent of participants feel more in control of work and life, and 97.4 percent of participants say they are more productive.

Filling the Leadership Gap

But what I have also discovered is that in the day-to-day operations at their organizations, some employees experience strong cultural resistance when implementing what they learn. When the senior leadership is not involved in the training, the impact on the overall organization (and therefore the return on the company's training investment) is not as powerful as it could be. Identifying that deficiency was my catalyst for *Work Without Walls* and the associated training for leadership.

Earlier in this chapter I recommended putting one leader in charge of intentional improvements related to each of the subjects tackled in this book. Even if you proceed with that model, you need to identify who will have ultimate responsibility for both individual and corporate productivity. I would call this role Chief Productivity Officer. Other experts advocate for a similar role, but they approach it from a slightly different angle. Tony Schwarz, noted business thinker and CEO of The Energy Project, discusses a Chief Energy Officer, because "the way you're feeling at any given moment profoundly influences how the people who work for you feel. How they're feeling, in turn, profoundly influences how well they perform."[111]

There has also been much discussion in the media regarding a Chief Happiness Officer. The impetus may have started with the wild success of Zappos, whose CEO, Tony Hsieh, views "happiness as a business model." In this model, the role of the Chief Happiness Officer (according to the current CHO at Zappos, Jenn Lim) is defined as "doing what any CEO does in an organization—putting the people/resources/financing in place to create a sustainable company. The difference between a CEO and a CHO is that a CHO is doing it through the lens of happiness as a business model."[112]

Regardless of what you call the role of the person who has ultimate responsibility, the focus is the same: maximizing the inputs and improving the outcomes related to the intangible qualities of knowledge work.

I urge you to consider putting one person in charge of these policies and their execution, and the job belongs to the CEO. Whether you refer to these issues collectively as related to energy, happiness, or productivity, they all have a major impact on the culture, and the culture starts at the top.

> **The CEO needs to be the Chief Productivity Officer.**

Therefore, the CEO must be the one to prevent unhealthy, distracted, "always-on" behaviors from thwarting a culture of success.

- -

Conclusion

Being intentional about knowledge worker productivity creates an environment where employees feel happy, engaged, and motivated rather than scattered, distracted, and overwhelmed. It provides the space for them to best apply their unique knowledge, experience, and talents, which are the reasons you hired them in the first place. When you're intentional about your culture, you improve the well-being and productivity of your staff—and the company as a whole.

- -

Action Items

These are specific steps that will help you put the information in this chapter to use immediately. Most can be implemented relatively quickly and easily and can pay big returns:

1. Using the figures provided in this chapter, estimate the cost of distractions to your organization.

2. Review the issues from previous chapters in *Work Without Walls* and pick the top three that you think are having the biggest impact on your organization. Have the rest of your leadership do the same, and compare your results.

3. Assign one leader to develop a plan, with estimated budget, to address those issues you determine to be the most important.

4. Assess leadership behaviors and practices that contribute to these top three issues, and make improving them part of each leader's annual plan.

5. Before rolling out any plans, determine how you will clearly communicate new expectations to employees.

6. Together with other leaders, identify your desired outcomes for each role in your company, as well as the inputs that affect how well workers deliver those results. Do this same exercise for your company as a whole.

7. If you're the CEO, take on the role of Chief Productivity Officer, and focus on driving a culture that supports success. If you're not the CEO, you can benefit the organization by bringing up at a leadership meeting the topic of responsibility for the culture of productivity.

- -

💬 Takeaways You Can Tweet

Here are important points of the chapter summarized so that they are easy to digest, but also so that you can conveniently share the information with your followers on Twitter or on other social media outlets. Follow and participate in the conversation online using *#workwithout-walls*, and/or my handle, @mnthomas.

❑ Workplace cultures that support productivity don't just happen; they require intention.

- ❑ Distraction sabotages productivity and hurts your bottom line.

- ❑ To make an office culture more productive, leaders have to change their own habits first.

- ❑ You'll send the strongest message when leaders model productive behaviors.

- ❑ To improve productivity in knowledge work, get clear on the most important results for each job role.

- ❑ The CEO should also be the Chief Productivity Officer and own the job of cultivating a healthy, productive environment.

Acknowledgments

I FIND my motivation for writing by waiting until I have something to share that I feel is important and useful. After my first book, it took me a long time to get to the point where I had a second book's worth of things to say. So many people have been involved in helping me develop and hone these ideas and assemble them in a way that was organized, logical, and useful.

Shortly after my first book came out, I started speaking for Vistage International. Working with these CEOs and senior executives gave me more insight into how my knowledge of personal productivity is important and useful at the corporate level. I value my experience with Vistage and appreciate every chairperson who has invited me to speak and the many Vistage members who have engaged with my message.

This book originally started out as an article that kept getting longer and longer. My friends and colleagues Sarah Beckham and Jenny Magic; my mom, Rita Kerins; and my husband, Shawn Thomas, were crucial in the early stages of this content. Thank you all so much for your dedication to my success, your support of my work, and your invaluable feedback. I appreciate you very much!

Kristen Taylor and Sarah Carmichael at *Harvard Business Review* took a chance on me for HBR's online outlet, which helped me test the content. Those articles are excerpts from this book, so Sarah's editing is also evident here. I appreciate both of you for your input, trust, and support.

My editor, Charlotte Kughen, agreed to work with me a second time, and this book is exponentially better for her involvement. Because it was in development for so long, I thought I needed a fresh set of eyes to view the book in its entirety, and Charlotte is also responsible for connecting me with Jennifer Lynn. Jennifer's involvement at the end of the process helped me with the last pieces I needed to make this final result something of which I'm immensely proud, but more importantly, something I feel will be exceptionally useful to my current and future clients. Thank you both for your careful deliberation and supportive feedback.

The staff at Jenkins Group, especially Yvonne Roehler, Leah Nicholson, and Elizabeth Chenette were the final piece in helping me get this book into your hands, and I appreciate their production assistance and advice.

Finally, my friend and talented designer Stephanie Johnson was instrumental in helping to express my ideas graphically, which I think is important and is also a skill that I most definitely don't have.☺

"ACCESS ECONOMY" COMPANIES

NOTE: This list should not be construed as an endorsement of these companies, but merely as a starting point for your own research.

All-Purpose Services

TaskRabbit: www.taskrabbit.com

As of this writing, TaskRabbit is available in nineteen cities: Atlanta, Austin, Boston, Chicago, Dallas, Denver, Houston, Los Angeles/Orange County, London, Miami, New York City, Philadelphia, Phoenix, Portland, San Antonio, San Diego, Seattle, San Francisco Bay Area, and Washington DC.

Use TaskRabbit by choosing from a list of popular chores and errands, or enter your own. Virtual tasks can also be done. They'll connect you with a Tasker within minutes of your request. Your Tasker arrives, completes the job, and bills directly in the app. The Taskers undergo what the company calls an "extensive vetting process" and all jobs are insured up to $1 million. There is no charge to post requests.

Thumbtack: www.thumbtack.com

This service helps you find someone to provide everything from photo shoots to singing lessons to organic house cleaning, and they claim to have providers in all fifty states.

To use Thumbtack, you fill out a survey about what type of service provider you're looking for. You'll be sent up to five quotes within hours to compare prices, profiles, and reviews, and then you select a provider. There is no charge to post requests.

NeedTo: www.needto.com

NeedTo has an altruistic bent and provides virtual services anywhere, but the specific locations where it can provide services is unclear from the website. They are based in Austin, Texas. Like TaskRabbit, they cover a wide variety of needs, from household repairs and chores to office workers and writers. The altruism is indicated in their mission statement: "NeedTo helps fulfill the American dream by providing a platform to those who dream of working for themselves, yet at the same time provides small business steady work. So what about the person who wants to work but lacks the skills? NeedTo pledges 10% of all profits to local non-profits who specialize in job skills training—a worthwhile investment towards our mission to give all those who want to work, a reliable place to find it." There is no charge to post requests.

Hello Alfred: www.helloalfred.com

This site "pairs busy individuals (a.k.a. you) with organized, knowledgeable, intuitive people who handle all of life's necessities: from groceries and dry cleaning, to tailoring and sending packages . . . providers are willing to do almost anything, as long as it's legal." Unique about this site is that their workers are hired as full-time employees, rather than contract workers, and they are offered health benefits. It also uses other sites listed here as subcontractors. Fees are based on the number of services per week. Hello Alfred is currently available in the following five cities: Boston, Brooklyn, Los Angeles, New York, and San Francisco.

Yelp: www.yelp.com

Once an online destination to provide restaurant reviews, Yelp now provides reviews on a variety of businesses including home improvement professionals, salons and other personal care services, and stores.

NextDoor: www.nextdoor.com

NextDoor is "the private social network for your neighborhood." It is a way for people to stay on top of what is happening in their own neighborhoods, including hearing the latest news about such things as block parties, or recent crime. Local police departments are using NextDoor to share community information. Neighbors can also communicate with each other and post recommendations and referrals for local service providers.

BarterSugar: www.bartersugar.com

This company is unique to this list. It is geared to startup companies, and very small businesses, and offers a platform where businesses can trade, or "barter," goods or services to get what they need without paying for it. A business can register to be listed for free, and the cost to complete the barter is 7.5 percent of the estimated worth of the item or service. BarterSugar says they are global but can help you find what you need locally.

Business/Office/Technology Services

Upwork: www.upwork.com

Upwork is the result of a merger between Elance and ODesk and offers professional services providers such as web developers, virtual assistants, customer service reps, writers, programmers, and accountants. Upwork has service plans for posting requests that are both free and fee-based.

Fancy Hands: www.fancyhands.com

Fancy Hands primarily offers short tasks from virtual assistants, such as research. There is a nominal fee to use the site, but it goes toward the cost of the services you use.

Perssist: www.perssist.com

Also provides remote personal assistants for tasks such as research, making calls, making reservations and appointments, event planning, and doing short personal tasks. In their own words, they offer: "Anything an intelligent, Internet-savvy liberal arts major with a long-distance calling plan can do, we can do." Therefore they don't offer services that are very technical or require professional training, such as coding or accounting.

VirtualAssistants.com: www.virtualassistants.com

This site specializes in work at home jobs in customer service, secretarial, regular transcription, medical transcription, coding, captioning, research, writing, editing, proofreading, social media, blogging, administrative, email support, reservation agents, WordPress help, telemarketing, sales, help desk, tech support, technical, "and other real virtual assistant jobs." There is a nominal fee to use the site, and they say that they pre-screen jobs.

Virtual Assist USA: www.virtualassistusa.com

Virtual Assist USA offers services such as administrative, marketing, web design, graphic design, social media marketing, search engine optimization, copywriting, content development, video editing, and business consulting. They offer a team approach, including your own project manager. They offer three client plans including a pay-as-you-go option, and a project-based option. Their providers work in your office.

Home Repair and Improvement

HomeAdvisor: www.homeadvisor.com

A website to find professionals for home maintenance, everything from architects to handyman services to home security, and more. It's free to use the site, and you start by answering a few questions about your project. HomeAdvisor then sends you information for up to four pre-screened, local home improvement providers. HomeAdvisor started out as ServiceMagic.

Pro Referral: www.proreferral.com

This site is "powered by Home Depot" and offers a referral service for a variety of home service and improvement jobs. It's free to use and was started as RedBeacon.

Grocery and Meal Services

PrepDish: www.prepdish.com

PrepDish is a subscription-based meal-planning service, offering monthly or yearly subscriptions that provide you with meal plans plus printable grocery lists and prep lists. All meals offered are gluten-free, paleo, and created by a professional chef.

The Fresh 20: www.thefresh20.com

Similar to PrepDish, this service offers five different types of meal plans they call classic, gluten-free, vegetarian, paleo, or meals for one. It offers monthly, quarterly, and annual subscriptions. Each week's meals are based on a list of twenty in-season ingredients.

Plated: www.plated.com

Plated goes a step beyond the meal plans and sends not only the recipes but also delivers the ingredients to your door. It provides weekly plans for "dinner for two," and they offer vegetarian, meat, and seafood choices. They have this to say about the quality of their food: "Our ingredients are sourced locally whenever possible, and are always carefully curated from responsible providers. While we don't exclusively source organically, we use 100% domestic and sustainably sourced seafood, 100% antibiotic-free meats, beef with no added hormones, and produce that is fresh, seasonal, and hand-packed." Ingredients come pre-measured and pre-packaged.

Blue Apron: blueapron.com

This service is similar to Plated but also offers a family plan. Shipping is included, and you can skip or cancel any time. Delivery is nationwide, and you can preview menus in advance.

Hello Fresh: hellofresh.com

Similar to Plated and Blue Apron but involves celebrity chef and restaurateur Jamie Oliver. Also, a portion of the proceeds of each meal ordered goes to Jamie's Food Foundation, an education-based organization to help children learn more about eating healthy foods.

Instacart: www.instacart.com

Instacart is a grocery delivery service. You order your groceries online from a store of your choice, and someone from Instacart delivers within an hour. They also offer recipes with lists of ingredients for you to order and have delivered. One important note: Instacart uses their own prices for your grocery items, not the store's prices. As of this writing, it is available in select cities in the following eighteen states: California, Colorado, Connecticut, Florida, Georgia, Illinois, Indiana, Maryland, Massachusetts, Michigan, Minnesota, New Jersey, New York, North Carolina, Oregon, Pennsylvania, Texas, Virginia, Washington, and Washington DC.

FURTHER READING

FOR further learning, education, and resources on the topics presented in this book, please contact me regarding consulting, training, or speaking services at maura@regainyourtime.com or 424-226-2872. For independent learning, the resources listed here will be helpful.

You can find links to these and more at RegainYourTime.com/Research-Resources.

Books

Achor, Shawn. *The Happiness Advantage: The Seven Principles of Positive Psychology That Fuel Success and Performance at Work*

Chapman, Bob and Sisodia, Raj. *Everybody Matters: The Extraordinary Power of Caring for Your People Like Family*

Gelles, David. *Mindful Work: How Meditation Is Changing Business from the Inside Out*

Goleman, Daniel. *Focus: The Hidden Driver of Excellence*

Hallowell, Edward. *CrazyBusy: Overstretched, Overbooked, and About to Snap! Strategies for Handling Your Fast-Paced Life*

Hsieh, Tony. *Delivering Happiness: A Path to Profits, Passion, and Purpose*

Huffington, Arianna. *Thrive: The Third Metric to Redefining Success and Creating a Life of Well-Being, Wisdom, and Wonder*

Newport, Cal. *Deep Work: Rules for Focused Success in a Distracted World*

Ratey, John. *Spark: The Revolutionary New Science of Exercise and the Brain*

Schwartz, Tony, Gomes, Jean, and McCarthy, Catherine. *The Way We're Working Isn't Working: The Four Forgotten Needs That Energize Great Performance*

Thomas, Maura Nevel. *Personal Productivity Secrets: Do what you never thought possible with your time and attention...and regain control of your life!* (my first book)

Turkle, Sherry. *Reclaiming Conversation: The Power of Talk in a Digital Age*

Reports, Periodicals, and Research

Center for Democracy & Technology. "Risk at Home: Privacy and Security Risks in Telecommuting." Presented by Ernst & Young. https://cdt.org/files/privacy/20080729_riskathome.pdf.

Drucker, Peter. "Knowledge-Worker Productivity: The Biggest Challenge." *California Management Review*, Vol. 41, No. 2, Winter 1999. http://www.forschungsnetzwerk.at/downloadpub/knowledge_workers_the_biggest_challenge.pdf.

"The Privacy Crisis." *Steelcase 360 Magazine*, Issue 68. www.steelcase.com/privacy.

Project: Time Off. Powered by the U.S. Travel Association. www.projecttimeoff.com.

World Green Building Council. "Health, Wellbeing & Productivity in Offices: The Next Chapter for Green Building." http://www.worldgbc.org/files/6314/1152/0821/WorldGBC__Health_Wellbeing__productivity_Full_Report.pdf.

APPS, TOOLS, AND OTHER RESOURCES

T HIS is in no way an exhaustive list, nor should inclusion on this list be considered an endorsement. A detailed description or comparison of each of these tools in a book is difficult because features and pricing are constantly changing. My suggestion, should you want more information, would be to do an Internet search for the tool or for a comparison between tools, but limit your search criteria to the prior six to twelve months. (In Google, this is done with the "Search Tools" option located just under the search box.)

Employee Feedback

15five (15five.com): An employee feedback system providing an automated and fast weekly check-in with every employee. It does not provide anonymous feedback, but rather it offers a way to spot problems, recognize employees, and gauge engagement.

TINYpulse (tinypulse.com): An employee feedback system with a focus on measuring how happy, burned out, and frustrated employees are. Feedback is anonymous but also offers the opportunity for recognition and suggestions.

Happiness At Work Survey (happinessatworksurvey.com): A more extensive survey that offers deeper insights into corporate well-being.

Video and Group Communication Tools

Google Hangouts (hangouts.google.com): A communication platform that offers instant messaging and one-on-one or group video chat.

Skype (skype.com): A communication platform owned by Microsoft that offers video, voice call, and instant messenger services, domestically and internationally.

Note: Google Hangouts and Skype are very similar. Google Hangouts seems to be used more frequently by individuals and Skype seems to be used more frequently for business communication.

HipChat (hipchat.com): An internal chat application that offers one-on-one and group chat in a way that makes internal public conversations searchable and accessible to anyone in the organization.

Slack (slack.com): An internal messaging, group chat, and document sharing application similar to an internal social media platform.

Yammer (yammer.com): An enterprise social networking service for private communication inside organizations, owned by Microsoft.

Note: All three of these tools are very similar and serve the same need.

Email Management Tools

MailButler (feingeist.io/mailbutler): A "personal assistant for Apple Mail," this tool offers reminder, tracking, scheduling, and other services for incoming and outgoing email messages.

Boomerang (boomeranggmail.com): Offers similar features of MailButler but only for Gmail.

SpamDrain (spamdrain.com): A filtering service for individual and domain-level email accounts. Requires access to your email account.

Throttle (throttlehq.com): A service offered by browser extension that generates unique email addresses for everything you use online; so you can control who sends you email and when. Does not require access to your email account. (Read my review and recommendation at regain-yourtime.com/email-management-tool-review-throttle)

Unroll Me (unroll.me): A service that offers easy unsubscribe and filtering of email messages. Requires access to your email account.

Note: SpamDrain, Throttle, and Unroll Me are similar services with the notable exception that Throttle does not require access to your email account; however, it does not immediately apply to your existing email subscriptions unless you manually change them.

Co-Working Spaces

LExC (lexc.com): A network of independent co-working spaces with "common standards of excellence."

Regus (regus.com): Short and long-term executive suite rental that also offers receptionist, admin, and tech support services.

WeWork (wework.com): Called by its founder a "physical social network," provides access to local work spaces but also memberships to work at other spaces throughout the world. Locations also serve as social hangouts after hours.

Note: This is just a partial list of co-working businesses that have multiple locations. Most urban areas throughout the world have independent co-working spaces with various levels of amenities.

Meditation/Mindfulness Tools

Buddhify (buddhify.com): Meditation app for iOS and Android devices offering guided meditations of various lengths, grouped by their relevance to a particular activity or situation, such as "taking a break from work," "being in nature," or "dealing with difficult emotions."

Calm (calm.com): Meditation app for browsers, iOS and Android devices. Offers white noise and tranquil imagery, timed, open-ended, and guided meditations, plus daily programs such as "21 Days of Calm."

Focus@Will (focusatwill.com): Provides audio soundtracks that "combine neuroscience and music to boost productivity and tune out distractions."

Endnotes

Introduction

1   Elaine Pofeldt, "Shocker: 40% of Workers Now Have 'Contingent' Jobs, Says U.S. Government," *Forbes*, May 25, 2015, http://www.forbes.com/sites/elainepofeldt/2015/05/25/shocker-40-of-workers-now-have-contingent-jobs-says-u-s-government/#3837cb2a2532

2   Ron Carucci, "A 10-Year Study Reveals What Great Executives Know and Do," *Harvard Business Review*, January 19, 2016, https://hbr.org/2016/01/a-10-year-study-reveals-what-great-executives-know-and-do

3   Dan Lyons, "Congratulations! You've Been Fired," *New York Times*, April 9, 2016, http://www.ny-times.com/2016/04/10/opinion/sunday/congratulations-youve-been-fired.html

Chapter 1: The "Human" Part of Human Capital

4   Peter F. Drucker, "Knowledge-Worker Productivity: The Biggest Challenge," *California Management Review*, Winter 1999, Vol. 41, No. 2, http://forschungsnetzwerk.at/downloadpub/knowledge_work-ers_the_biggest_challenge.pdf

5   Alexander Caillet, Jeremy Hirschberg, and Stefano Petti, "How Your State of Mind Affects Your Performance," *Harvard Business Review*, December 8, 2014, https://hbr.org/2014/12/how-your-state-of-mind-affects-your-performance

6   Tony Schwartz and Christine Porath, "Why You Hate Work," *New York Times*, May 30, 2014, http://www.nytimes.com/2014/06/01/opinion/sunday/why-you-hate-work.html?_r=1

7   Travis Bradberry, "Critical Things Ridiculously Successful People Do Every Day," LinkedIn Pulse, April 7, 2016, https://www.linkedin.com/pulse/critical-things-ridiculously-successful-people-do-every-bradberry

8   Jennifer Gibson, "Blood Glucose and the Brain: Sugar and Short-Term Memory," *Brain Blogger*, June 26, 2008, http://brainblogger.com/2008/06/26/blood-glucose-and-the-brain-sugar-and-short-term-memory/

9   "Insufficient Sleep Is a Public Health Problem," Centers for Disease Control and Prevention, http://www.cdc.gov/features/dssleep/

10   Nick va Dam and Els van der Helm, "The Organizational Cost of Insufficient Sleep," *McKinsey Quarterly*, February 2016, http://www.mckinsey.com/business-functions/organization/our-insights/the-organizational-cost-of-insufficient-sleep

11   Nicole Torres, "Survey: How Does Late-Night Emailing Affect You?" *Harvard Business Review*, April 17, 2015, https://hbr.org/2015/04/survey-how-does-late-night-emailing-affect-you

12   Sarah Klein, "6 Convincing Reasons to Take a Nap Today," *Huffington Post*, March 11, 2013, http://www.huffingtonpost.com/2013/03/11/nap-benefits-national-napping-day_n_2830952.html

13   Annie Hauser and Allison Takeda, "The Most Sleep-Friendly Companies in America," *Everyday Health*, March 2, 2012, http://www.everydayhealth.com/sleep-pictures/the-most-sleep-friendly-companies-in-america.aspx

14   "Workplace Stress," American Institute of Stress, http://www.stress.org/workplace-stress/

15   Chris Mossa, "Stop Stressing, Get Happy, and Watch Your Work Performance Turn Around," *WNYC Money Talking*, March 19, 2015, http://www.wnyc.org/story/stop-stressing-get-happy-watch-work-performance-turn-around/

16   "Stop Stressing, Get Happy, and Watch Your Work Performance Turn Around," PodCastOne, Money Talking, http://www.podcastone.com/pg/jsp/program/episode.jsp?programID=735&pid=493466.

17   "Mindfulness," *Psychology Today*, https://www.psychologytoday.com/basics/mindfulness

18 Christina Congleton, Britta K. Hölzel, and Sara W. Lazar, "Mindfulness Can Literally Change Your Brain," *Harvard Business Review*, January 8, 2015, https://hbr.org/2015/01/mindfulness-can-literally-change-your-brain

19 Jeanne Meister, "Future of Work: Mindfulness as a Leadership Practice," *Forbes*, April 27, 2015, http://www.forbes.com/sites/jeannemeister/2015/04/27/future-of-work-mindfulness-as-a-leadership-practice/#5e49a670a41b

20 Cynthia Ramnarance, "Why You Need to Have a Hobby," *Business Insider*, March 12, 2014, http://www.businessinsider.com/why-you-need-to-have-a-hobby-2014-3

21 Thai Nguyen, "Hacking into Your Happy Chemicals: Dopamine, Serotonin, Endorphins and Oxytocin," *Huffington Post*, October 20, 2014, http://www.huffingtonpost.com/thai-nguyen/hacking-into-your-happy-c_b_6007660.html

22 Arjun Dev Arora and Raman Frey, "A Manager's Job Is Making Sure Employees Have a Life Outside Work," *Harvard Business Review*, March 25, 2016, https://hbr.org/2016/03/a-managers-job-is-making-sure-employees-have-a-life-outside-work

23 Sara Robinson, "Why We Have to Go Back to a 40-Hour Work Week to Keep Our Sanity," AlterNet, March 13, 2012, http://www.alternet.org/story/154518/why_we_have_to_go_back_to_a_40-hour_work_week_to_keep_our_sanity

24 Harry Levinson, "When Executives Burn Out," *Harvard Business Review*, July-August 1996, https://hbr.org/1996/07/when-executives-burn-out

25 Clayton M. Christensen, "How Will You Measure Your Life?" *Harvard Business Review*, July-August 2010. https://hbr.org/2010/07/how-will-you-measure-your-life?

26 Julian Birkinshaw and Jordan Cohen, "Make Time for the Work That Matters," *Harvard Business Review*, September 2013, https://hbr.org/2013/09/make-time-for-the-work-that-matters

27 Melba J. Duncan, "The Case for Executive Assistants," *Harvard Business Review*, May 2011, https://hbr.org/2011/05/the-case-for-executive-assistants

28 Giana M. Eckhardt and Fleura Bardhi, "The Sharing Economy Isn't About Sharing at All," *Harvard Business Review*, January 28, 2015, https://hbr.org/2015/01/the-sharing-economy-isnt-about-sharing-at-all

29 Claire Schooley, "Drive Employee Talent Development Through Business Mentoring Programs," Forrester Research, August 6, 2010, http://www.bu.edu/questrom/files/2013/07/Forrester-Research-Report-Drive-Employee-Talent-Development-Through-Business-Mentoring-Programs.pdf

30 Tony Schwartz and Christine Porath, "Your Boss's Work-Life Balance Matters as Much as Your Own," *Harvard Business Review*, July 10, 2014, https://hbr.org/2014/07/your-bosss-work-life-balance-matters-as-much-as-your-own

Chapter 2: Distraction, Attention, and the Twenty-First Century Work Culture

31 Herbert A. Simon, "Designing Organizations for an Information-Rich World," in Martin Greenberger, *Computers, Communication, and the Public Interest* (Baltimore, MD: Johns Hopkins Press, 1971), pages 40–41.

32 Eric Matson and Laurence Prusack, "Boosting the Productivity of Knowledge Workers," *McKinsey Quarterly*, September 2010, http://www.mckinsey.com/insights/organization/boosting_the_productivity_of_knowledge_workers

33 Maria Konnikova, "The Open-Office Trap," *The New Yorker*, January 7, 2014, http://www.newyorker.com/business/currency/the-open-office-trap

34 Bruce N. Pfau, "What Do Millennials Really Want at Work? The Same Things the Rest of Us Do," *Harvard Business Review*, April 7, 2016, https://hbr.org/2016/04/what-do-millennials-really-want-at-work

35 Paul Hammerness and Margaret Moore, "Train Your Brain to Focus," *Harvard Business Review*, January 18, 2012, https://hbr.org/2012/01/train-your-brain-to-focus

36 GSA Enterprise Transformations, "Knowledge Worker Productivity: Challenges, Issues, Solutions," June 2011, page 3, http://www.gsa.gov/graphics/admin/KnowledgeWorkerProductivity_Final6811.pdf

37 Martin Zwilling, "How to Increase Productivity by Employee Happiness," *Forbes*, December 2, 2014, http://www.forbes.com/sites/martinzwilling/2014/12/02/how-to-squeeze-productivity-from-employee-happiness/

38 Adam Gorlick, "Media Multitaskers Pay Mental Price, Stanford Study Shows," *Stanford News*, August 24, 2009, http://news.stanford.edu/news/2009/august24/multitask-research-study-082409.html

39 Maura Thomas, "Approach of Empowered Productivity: It's Not Really Time Management Training," Regain Your Time, http://www.regainyourtime.com/productivity-time-management-training/attention-management/productivity-training/

Chapter 3: The Challenge of Email and the Dangers of Constant Communication

40 Maura Thomas, "Fixing Our Unhealthy Obsession with Work Email," *Harvard Business Review*, September 24, 2015, https://hbr.org/2015/09/fixing-our-unhealthy-obsession-with-work-email

41 Robert M. Sapolsky, "The Benefits of Mind-Wandering," the *Wall Street Journal*, June 19, 2015, http://www.wsj.com/articles/the-benefits-of-mind-wandering-1434716243

42 "Take Notes by Hand for Better Long-Term Comprehension," Association for Psychological Science, http://www.psychologicalscience.org/index.php/news/releases/take-notes-by-hand-for-better-long-term-comprehension.html

43 "Is Multitasking More Efficient? Shifting Mental Gears Costs Time, Especially When Shifting to Less Familiar Tasks," American Psychological Association, August 5, 2001, http://www.umich.edu/~bcalab/articles/APAPressRelease2001.pdf

44 Cal Newport, "A Modest Proposal: Eliminate Email," *Harvard Business Review*, February 18, 2016, https://hbr.org/2016/02/a-modest-proposal-eliminate-email

45 Tom Parisi, "Workplace Telepressure: NIU Researchers: Why Preoccupation with Work Emails, Texts Could Be Bad for Your Health," Northern Illinois University, http://www.niu.edu/features/11-13-14/telepressure.shtml

46 Ferris Jabr, "Why Your Brain Needs More Downtime," *Scientific American*, October 15, 2013, http://www.scientificamerican.com/article/mental-downtime/

47 Gaia Grant, "Boosting the Brain's Creative Powers & Creating the Best Environment for Innovation," *Innovation Management*, April 30, 2014, http://www.innovationmanagement.se/2014/04/30/boosting-the-brains-creative-powers-creating-the-best-environment-for-innovation/

48 Tony Schwartz and Christine Porath, "Why You Hate Work," *New York Times*, May 30, 2014, http://www.nytimes.com/2014/06/01/opinion/sunday/why-you-hate-work.html?_r=1

49 Margaret Wheeler Johnson, "Burnout Is Everywhere—Here's What Countries Are Doing to Fix It," *Huffington Post*, August 1, 2013, http://www.huffingtonpost.com/2013/07/30/worker-burnout-worldwide-governments_n_3678460.html

50 Neil Irwin, "How Some Men Fake an 80-Hour Workweek, and Why It Matters," *New York Times*, May 4, 2015, http://www.nytimes.com/2015/05/05/upshot/how-some-men-fake-an-80-hour-workweek-and-why-it-matters.html?_r=2

Chapter 4: Is Your Vacation Policy Broken?

51 John Donahoe, "To Beat the Chaos, Take a Thinking Day," LinkedIn Pulse, July 15, 2013, https://www.linkedin.com/pulse/20130715110232-187399433-to-beat-the-chaos-take-a-thinking-day

52 Wednesday Martin, "Gone Fishin': Why You Can't Afford to Skip Another Vacation," *Psychology Today*, July 7, 2010, https://www.psychologytoday.com/blog/stepmonster/201007/gone-fishin-why-you-cant-afford-skip-another-vacation

53 Shawn Achor, "Are the People Who Take Vacations the Ones Who Get Promoted?" *Harvard Business Review*, June 12, 2015, https://hbr.org/2015/06/are-the-people-who-take-vacations-the-ones-who-get-promoted

54 "Project Time Off Research Overview." Project: Time Off, http://www.projecttimeoff.com/sites/default/files/P.TO_Research_FactSheet_0.pdf

55 Ibid.

56 Daniel H. Pink, "Netflix Lets Its Staff Take as Much Holiday as They Want, Whenever They Want—and It Works" The Telegraph, August 14, 2010, http://www.telegraph.co.uk/finance/newsbysector/mediatechnologyandtelecoms/7945719/Netflix-lets-its-staff-take-as-much-holiday-as-they-want-whenever-they-want-and-it-works.html

57 Richard Branson, "Why We're Letting Virgin Staff Take as Much Holiday as They Want," *Virgin Newsletter*, September 23, 2014, http://www.virgin.com/richard-branson/why-were-letting-virgin-staff-take-as-much-holiday-as-they-want

58 Jonathan Chew, "Why Unlimited Vacation May Sound Better Than It Really Is," Fortune, March 10, 2016, http://fortune.com/2016/03/10/best-companies-unlimited-vacation/

59 Jeanne Sahadi, "Tribune Reverses Course on Unlimited Vacation Policy," *CNN Money*, November 24, 2014, http://money.cnn.com/2014/11/24/pf/tribune-vacation-policy/index.html?iid=EL.ht

60 "All Work and No Pay Impact Forfeited Time," Project: Time Off, http://www.projecttimeoff.com/research/all-work-and-no-pay-impact-forfeited-time

61 Glassdoor "Average U.S. Employee Only Takes Half of Earned Vacation Time; Glassdoor Employment Confidence Survey (Q1 2014)," April 3, 2014, www.glassdoor.com/blog/average-employee-takes-earned-vacation-time-glassdoor-employment-confidence-survey-q1-2014/

62 "Overwhelmed America: Why Don't We Use Our Earned Leave?" U.S. Travel Association, August 2014, http://www.projecttimeoff.com/sites/default/files/PTO_OverwhelmedAmerica_Report.pdf

63 Ibid.

64 Laura Waitz, "How to Be a Pro-Vacation Manager in a High-Pressure Industry," *Harvard Business Review*, June 22, 2015, https://hbr.org/2015/06/how-to-be-a-pro-vacation-manager-in-a-high-pressure-industry

65 John Donahoe, "To Beat the Chaos, Take a Thinking Day," LinkedIn Pulse, July 15, 2013, https://www.linkedin.com/pulse/20130715110232-187399433-to-beat-the-chaos-take-a-thinking-day

66 "Running a Small Business Is No Vacation," OnDeck, August 13, 2014, https://www.ondeck.com/company/in-the-news/press-releases/running-small-business-vacation-ondeck-study-finds/

67 Bob Chapman, "What Is Truly Human Leadership?" Truly Human Leadership, www.trulyhuman-leadership.com/?page_id=36

68 Jared Brown, "You Can Achieve Work-Life Balance as an Entrepreneur (Even with a Newborn)," *Forbes*, August 12, 2015, http://www.forbes.com/sites/theyec/2015/08/12/you-can-achieve-work-life-balance-as-an-entrepreneur-even-with-a-newborn/2/#3c67dda34522

69 "Should Holiday Email Be Deleted?" *BBC Magazine*, August 14, 2014, http://www.bbc.com/news/magazine-28786117

70 Bart Lorang, "Paid Vacation? That's Not Cool. You Know What's Cool? Paid, PAID Vacation," Full Contact, July 10, 2012, https://www.fullcontact.com/blog/paid-paid-vacation/

Chapter 5: The Office Environment

71 Amit Ray, *Mindfulness: Living in the Moment, Living in the Breath* (Inner Light Publishers, 2015)

72 World Green Building Council, "Health, Wellbeing & Productivity in Offices: The Next Chapter for Green Building," http://www.worldgbc.org/files/6314/1152/0821/WorldGBC__Health_Wellbeing__productivity_Full_Report.pdf

73 Christine Congdon, Donna Flynn, and Melanie Redman, "Balancing 'We' and 'Me': The Best Collaborative Spaces Also Support Solitude," *Harvard Business Review*, October 2014, https://hbr.org/2014/10/balancing-we-and-me-the-best-collaborative-spaces-also-support-solitude

74 Tonya L. Smith-Jackson and Katherine W. Klein, "Open Plan Offices: Task Performance and Mental Workload," *Journal of Environmental Psychology*, Volume 29, Issue 2, June 2009, pages 279–289, http://www.sciencedirect.com/science/article/pii/S0272494408000728

75 Maria Konnikova, "The Open-Office Trap," *The New Yorker*, January 7, 2014, http://www.newyorker.com/business/currency/the-open-office-trap

76 Sarah Green Carmichael, "Research: Cubicles Are the Absolute Worst," *Harvard Business Review*, November 13, 2013, https://hbr.org/2013/11/research-cubicles-are-the-absolute-worst/

77 Lindsey Kaufman, "Google Got It Wrong. The Open-Office Trend Is Destroying the Workplace," *The Washington Post*, December 30, 2014, http://www.washingtonpost.com/posteverything/wp/2014/12/30/google-got-it-wrong-the-open-office-trend-is-destroying-the-workplace/?tid=sm_

78 Jason Feifer, "Offices for All! Why Open-Office Layouts Are Bad for Employees, Bosses, and Productivity," *Fast Company*, November 4, 2013, http://www.fastcompany.com/3019758/dialed/offices-for-all-why-open-office-layouts-are-bad-for-employees-bosses-and-productivity

79 Ronald Alsop, "The Victims of Open Offices Are Pushing Back," BBC, December 12, 2014, http://www.bbc.com/capital/story/20140911-open-office-victims-push-back

80 Matt Blodgett, "But Where Do People Work in This Office?" MattBlodgett.com, January 14, 2015, http://www.mattblodgett.com/2015/01/but-where-do-people-work-in-this-office.html?m=1

81 Ariel Schwartz, "You're Not Alone: Most People Hate Open Offices," *Fast Company*, November 20, 2013, www.fastcoexist.com/3021713/youre-not-alone-most-people-hate-open-offices

82 Ethan Bernstein, "The Transparency Trap," *Harvard Business Review*, October 2014, https://hbr.org/2014/10/the-transparency-trap

83 Christina Bodin Danielsson, Holendro Singh Chungkham, Cornelia Wuiff, and Hugo Westerlund, "Office Design's Impact on Sick Leave Rates," *Journal of Ergonomics*, Volume 57, Issue 2, November 22, 2013, pages 139–147, http://www.tandfonline.com/doi/full/10.1080/00140139.2013.871064

84 Shawn Achor and Michelle Gielan, "Make Yourself Immune to Secondhand Stress," *Harvard Business Review*, September 2, 2015, https://hbr.org/2015/09/make-yourself-immune-to-secondhand-stress

85 Gary W. Evans and Dana Johnson, "Stress and Open-Office Noise," *Journal of Applied Psychology*, Volume 85(5), October 2000, pages 779–783, http://psycnet.apa.org/journals/apl/85/5/779/

86 Michael Rugg and Mark A. W. Andrews, "How Does Background Noise Affect Our Concentration?" *Scientific American*, January 1, 2010, http://www.scientificamerican.com/article/ask-the-brains-background-noise/

87 Maura Thomas, "Unleash Your Genius: Conversation with Dr. John Dovidio of Yale, Part 5," Regain Your Time, http://regainyourtime.com/unleash-your-genius-dovidio-part-5/

88 Rebecca Greenfield, "Brainstorming Doesn't Work; Try This Technique Instead," *Fast Company*, July 29, 2014, http://www.fastcompany.com/3033567/agendas/brainstorming-doesnt-work-try-this-technique-instead

89 Maura Thomas, "Control Makes Me Happy," Regain Your Time, http://regainyourtime.com/control-makes-me-happy/

90 Alana G. DeLoach, Jeff Carter, and Jonas Braasch, "Tuning the Cognitive Environment: Sound Masking with 'Natural' Sounds in Open-Plan Offices," *Journal of the Acoustical Society of America*, Volume 137, Issue 4, 2015, http://scitation.aip.org/content/asa/journal/jasa/137/4/10.1121/1.4920363

91 Oliver Burkeman, "Even Short Engagements with Nature Boost Productivity," *The Guardian*, March 17, 2013, posted at Business Insider, http://www.businessinsider.com/nature-boosts-productivity-2013-3

92 Christopher Calisi and Justin Stout, "Stop Noise from Ruining Your Open Office," *Harvard Business Review*, March 16, 2015, https://hbr.org/2015/03/stop-noise-from-ruining-your-open-office

93 Sarah Klein, "6 Convincing Reasons to Take a Nap Today," *Huffington Post*, March 11, 2013, http://www.huffingtonpost.com/2013/03/11/nap-benefits-national-napping-day_n_2830952.html

Chapter 6: The Location of Work

94 Meghan M. Biro, "Telecommuting Is the Future of Work," *Forbes*, January 12, 2014, http://www.forbes.com/sites/meghanbiro/2014/01/12/telecommuting-is-the-future-of-work/#7e085a89758f

95 "Survey on Workplace Flexibility 2013," WorldatWork, October 2013, https://www.worldatwork.org/adimLink?id=73898

96 "2013 Report Card for America's Infrastructure," American Society of Civil Engineers, http://www.infrastructurereportcard.org/bridges/

97 "Pros and Cons," Global Workplace Analytics, 2015, http://globalworkplaceanalytics.com/pros-cons

98 Ibid.

99 "Telecommuting Increases Work Hours and Blurs Boundary Between Work and Home, New Study Shows," *University of Texas News*, December 3, 2012, http://www.utexas.edu/news/2012/12/03/telecommuting-increases-work-hours-blurs-boundary-between-work-home-new-study-shows/

100 Paul J. Zak, "The Power of a Handshake: How Touch Sustains Personal and Business Relationships," *Huffington Post*, October 30, 2008, http://www.huffingtonpost.com/paul-j-zak/the-power-of-a-handshake_b_129441.html

101 Center for Democracy & Technology, "Risk at Home: Privacy and Security Risks in Telecommuting," presented by Ernst & Young, 2008, https://cdt.org/files/privacy/20080729_riskathome.pdf

102 Allison Arieff, "People Are the Core," Dialogues with Densler, December 21, 2012, http://www.gensler.com/uploads/documents/People%20are%20the%20Core_12_21_2012.pdf

103 Rose Cahalan, "The Work-From-Home Wars," *The Alcalde*, July/August 2013, http://alcalde.texasexes.org/2013/06/the-work-from-home-wars/

104 Center for Democracy & Technology, "Risk at Home: Privacy and Security Risks in Telecommuting," presented by Ernst & Young, 2008, https://cdt.org/files/privacy/20080729_riskathome.pdf

Chapter 7: Intention and Improvement

105 Peter Drucker, *Management Challenges in the 21st Century* (New York: Harper Business, 1999), page 135.

106 Bob Sullivan and Hugh Thompson, "Brain, Interrupted," *New York Times*, May 3, 2013, http://www.nytimes.com/2013/05/05/opinion/sunday/a-focus-on-distraction.html

107 Kermit Pattison, "Worker, Interrupted: The Cost of Task Switching," *Fast Company*, July 28, 2008, http://www.fastcompany.com/944128/worker-interrupted-cost-task-switching

108 Peter Drucker, "Knowledge-Worker Productivity: The Biggest Challenge," *California Management Review*, Volume 41, Number 2, Winter 1999, page 87, http://www.forschungsnetzwerk.at/downloadpub/knowledge_workers_the_biggest_challenge.pdf

109 Ibid., page 86.

110 Shawn Achor, "Positive Intelligence," *Harvard Business Review*, January-February 2012, https://hbr.org/2012/01/positive-intelligence

111 Tony Schwartz, "The CEO Is the Chief Energy Officer," *Harvard Business Review*, June 2, 2010, https://hbr.org/2010/06/the-ceo-is-the-chief-energy-of-2/

112 "Jenn Lim, CEO & Co-Founder, Speaker, Professional Bio" Delivering Happiness, http://deliveringhappiness.com/team/jenn-lim/

About the Author

Maura nevel thomas

is an award-winning international speaker, trainer, and author on productivity, attention management, and work-life balance for companies such as Old Navy, AIG, and Dell. She is a TEDx speaker and founder of RegainYourTime.com. Her first book, *Personal Productivity Secrets*, has been called a "home run" and a "game changer." Maura is a favorite media source on these topics and is featured weekly in national outlets such as the *Wall Street Journal, Fast Company*, and *Inc.* She's also a regular contributor to the *Harvard Business Review*, where her debut article was among the most widely read on the site that year.

Maura is a Bostonian at heart but lives in Austin, Texas with her husband, Shawn, their three-legged dog, Elliot, and their neurotic cat, Cash.

Follow her on Twitter @mnthomas.

Index

RegainYourTime.com

— TURNING CHAOS INTO CONTROL —➔

MAURA NEVEL THOMAS travels the world training teams to reduce their stress and regain control over their work, and training leaders to create corporate environments that facilitate high-quality knowledge work. When she isn't delivering training, Maura is giving inspirational, educational, and humorous keynote presentations for corporate retreats, industry conferences, and other events. Here are some comments from her appreciative clients. Many more are available at regainyourtime.com.

"I am amazed at the changes in my life since taking your training and reading your book! I work less, I feel more in control, my stress has gone down, I sleep better, and I'm getting better results. It's changed not only my work life, but my personal life as well. My team is reporting similar results. Thank you so much!"

—DENISE VERDICCHIO, SENIOR DIRECTOR-PUBLIC SECTOR
SHI INTERNATIONAL CORP, NEW BRUNSWICK, NJ

"Maura's training was a game-changer for our organization!"

—RONDA RUTLEDGE, EXECUTIVE DIRECTOR
SUSTAINABLE FOOD CENTER, AUSTIN, TX

"I got so much out of last week's session. I feel much less stressed— what a difference! Thank you!"

—CHRIS WALDO, SENIOR MANAGER
VMWARE, INC., PALO ALTO, CA

"I was very impressed with your presentation. Overall it was excellent. It has changed my life and I am determined it will more so. My wife is also thankful!"

—JEFF DAVIS, CFO
PRESBYTERIAN SENIOR LIVING, HARRISBURG, PA

"Maura delivered a fantastic presentation! Her humor and enthusiasm kept us engaged and excited to learn all her strategies for productivity. We left the training feeling inspired, enlightened, and motivated . . . It's important to mention that Maura was also a pleasure to work with and eager to understand our business so that she could really connect on a deeper level with our employees. Thank you Maura!"

—ELLIE DELUCA, EDUCATION COORDINATOR
SALONCENTRIC, DIVISION OF L'OREAL, NEW YORK, NY

Maura can deliver content ranging from one hour to two full days. She is diligent about qualifying every client and customizing the content and the length to achieve your specific objectives.

**Learn more at RegainYourTime.com
or contact Maura directly at info@regainyourtime.com
or 424-226-2872.**

Empowered Productivity.